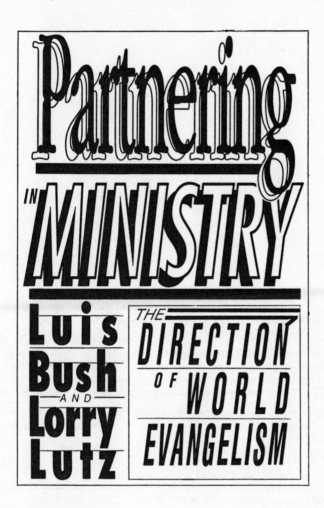

Partnering in MINISTRY

Luis Bush AND Lorry Lutz

THE DIRECTION OF WORLD EVANGELISM

INTERVARSITY PRESS
DOWNERS GROVE, ILLINOIS 60515

InterVarsity Press is the book-publishing division of InterVarsity Christian Fellowship, a student movement active on campus at hundreds of universities, colleges and schools of nursing in the United States of America, and a member movement of the International Fellowship of Evangelical Students. For information about local and regional activities, write Public Relations Dept., InterVarsity Christian Fellowship, 6400 Schroeder Rd., P.O. Box 7895, Madison, WI 53707-7895.

All Scripture quotations, unless otherwise indicated, are from the Holy Bible, New International Version. Copyright ©1973, 1978, International Bible Society. Used by permission of Zondervan Bible Publishers.

ISBN 0-8303-1332-2

Printed in the United States of America

Library of Congress Cataloging-in-Publication Data

Bush, Luis.
    Partnering in ministry: the direction of world evangelism/ Luis Bush & Lorry Lutz.
        p.   cm.
    ISBN 0-8308-1332-2
    1. Missions—Theory. 2. Partnership. 3. Indigenous church administration. I. Lutz, Lorry. II. Title.
    BV2063.B815   1990
    266—dc20   90-49872
                                                            CIP

15	14	13	12	11	10	9	8	7	6	5	4	3	2	1
01	00	99	98	97	96	95	94	93	92	91	90			

To our partner ministries
around the world who are patiently
and lovingly teaching
us how to be better partners

1 Partnerships Everywhere   *11*

The Growth of the Partnership Movement

2 Partnering Goes Back a Long Way   *21*

Biblical Roots

3 From Paternalism to Partnership   *34*

The Change in Missions Strategy

4 It Sounds Like a Marriage   *44*

Seeing Each Other As Equal Partners

5 Maintaining a Balance   *55*

Setting Up Accountability Structures

6 The Daughter Becomes a Friend   *70*

Founding Agencies Partnering with National Churches

7 Mainline Models   *79*

Denominational Partnerships

8 Crucified Nationalism   *87*

Partnership through International Teams

9 Great Expectations   *99*

Western Agencies with Indigenous National Ministries

10 Testing the Waters   *112*
    Two-Thirds World Partnerships

11 Increasing the Risk Factor   *126*
    Local Churches Take the Lead

12 Global Glue   *140*
    Worldwide Partnerships

13 Into the Next Century   *151*
    Partnership for A.D. 2000

14 Teaming Up to Give   *159*
    Bridging the Financial Gap

15 The Cords of Victory   *173*
    Is This Really a Partnership?

Appendix 1. **Partners International Sample Working Agreement** ____ *181*

Appendix 2. **Partner Mission Agreement between the Indian
Evangelical Mission and Sudan Interior Mission International** _____ *185*

Appendix 3. **Great Commission Manifesto** _____ *189*

Notes _____ *191*

Foreword

What is your place in world mission? What is God's will for you? How do you find the right mission agency? Probably you brought some of these questions to Urbana 90. They are big questions. Communicating to the world is an enormous job.

Good news! Jesus sent out the disciples in pairs. Ephesians speaks of believers working together as the body of Christ. The Philippians and Paul also modeled partnership in mission. We are not responsible for the whole job, only for our faithfulness.

In *Partnering in Ministry* you can explore the practical side of partnership in mission. Why do it? This book shows how partnership in mission is both biblical and relevant. It more than doubles our resources and effectiveness. You will enjoy stories from Luis Bush's years of experience partnering with Two-Thirds World churches and mission agencies. You will get tips on how to evaluate mission agencies—how well do they partner or work together on kingdom goals? You will learn something about practicing partnership.

Dan Harrison, director
InterVarsity Missions and Urbana

Preface

The heart of Christian partnership is fellowship. Christian fellowship is one of the most joyful and fulfilling experiences in life. It was this discovery in three areas that gave me the idea for this book on partnership. The three areas were partnership in marriage, partnership in the ministry of the apostle Paul with the Philippian church and partnership in my own ministry with Partners International, associating with over sixty "partner ministries" in almost fifty countries of the world.

The idea was born on January 30, 1989. I came home from the office and walked into a family set-up. Our four children, Jeanine, Stephanie, Naomi and Daniel, had collaborated with my wife, Doris, to re-enact our wedding eighteen years previous. My wedding band was quietly slipped off my finger. I was told to sit down, and suddenly the music started. Down the stairs came Doris in her wedding dress, followed by Stephanie and Naomi all dressed up. Then came Daniel, who acted as the ring bearer. Jeanine was the official photographer. After the exchange of vows led by Stephanie, they served sparkling cider. It was this evening of remembering our sweet partnership that prompted the thought of other Christian partnerships.

At the time, I was reading Paul's letter to the Philippian church and came to 1:4 where Paul describes his uncontainable joy because of his partnership with the church at Philippi. I felt the joy of discovery when I found in further study the multifaceted dimension of Christian partnership in the gospel. After five years with Partners International, I had become aware that, despite so many challenges of making ministry partnerships work, there was an increasingly joyful recognition that Christian partnerships *can* in fact work.

I consulted with my partner in ministry, Milan Telian, and our board member, Lois Curley, who both felt that this was a project worth pursuing. Almost two years later, as the project comes to completion, I am grateful to so many who partnered in the effort.

Lorry Lutz, senior writer and colleague in the ministry at Partners International, took on the task of writing the manuscript. It required interviewing many of those who collaborated generously with their own time and experiences, usually with refreshing candor, about their own partnerships.

Thanks to Derk Van Konynenburg, chairman of our international council; Keith Parks, president of the Foreign Mission Board of the Southern Baptist Convention; John Kyle, executive director of Mission to the World; Larry Keyes, president of OC Ministries International; Jim Montgomery, president of DAWN Ministries; Hugh Maclellan, Jr., of the Maclellan Foundation; Greg Ring, president of Dallas Seminary Foundation; Harold Fuller, deputy general director of SIM; and many others who have partnered in sharing the principles, joys and challenges of their own partnerships. Thanks also to Lois Curley who helped in the publication process. My hope and prayer is that you will discover the joy of Christian partnership in a new way in the process of reading this book.

Luis Bush, international president
Partners International/ Christian Nationals
Evangelism Commission (CNEC)

Chapter 1

Partnerships Everywhere

The San Joaquin Valley stretches three hundred miles down the center of California. Scientific irrigation, plenty of sunshine and a favorable state government climate have helped to make this one of the richest farming areas of the world. Succulent peaches grow in abundance, as do grapes, almonds, walnuts, cherries and pears. The manicured orchards, coddled with all the water they need (and no more), stand in rows as straight as an army on parade.

Farming here is big business . . . competitive big business with little room for failure or amateurs. Equipment costs run to the hundreds of thousands of dollars; staff and personnel fall under laws as rigid as any industry.

And it's risky business, for a frost in the blossom season or a rain during harvest can spell the difference between wealth and disaster.

Partnership for More Than the Bottom Line

Derk Van Konynenburg grew up with farming in his blood. His Dutch father developed fruit farms with the innate skills of a natural-born farmer; but even before Derk graduated from the university and joined his father, it had become obvious that farming could no longer be done the old-fashioned way.

When Derk's father retired, Derk realized he could not go it alone. He recalls:

I wanted freedom in life to be able to do things other than just farming. In order to do that, whoever was going to be in the management with me had to feel as responsible as I did.

So Derk began looking for a partner, someone who could fill in where he was weak, preferably an expert in water control, pest treatment and fertility. John Britton, a consultant in pest management and water control, seemed to fill the bill.

John was not a Christian when he started working with Derk as a consultant, but the two men enjoyed a good relationship. John recalls:

Derk was the first person who was bold enough to tell me that he was a Christian, and his lifestyle backed it up. We had many long talks out in the field about the Lord.

Through Derk's and others' influence, John became a Christian. John's commitment to Christ was just one of many requirements Derk was looking for in a good partner; but, once the men started talking partnership in earnest, they found many areas of agreement. As John says:

Partnership is not unlike the way you talk about a marriage. . . . Maybe the most difficult adjustment . . . is deciding who's responsible for what.

Once an agreement was reached, the two men started a new company, in a sense, leasing the property from Derk. Then they started all over, purchasing equipment and sharing equal benefits.

They decided to name their partnership Britton-Konynenburg

Farms simply because it was in alphabetical order. Though Derk is the more dominant in personality, they both share in all decisions.

Derk remembers one time when a salesman came up to him while he was doing some welding on a spray tank, asking, "Where's the boss? Where's Britton?" Before Derk could direct him to John, the man had spewed off a lot of derogatory remarks about bosses in general. Derk just grinned and sent him off to find "the boss."

After fourteen years, the two men believe more than ever in the value of partnership. Because of shared responsibilities and goals, they are free to give time to serve the Lord. John has often taken time off for involvement in his church. Derk serves as international board chairman of Partners International. He always consults with John before going to a board meeting or travelling overseas because they long ago made the commitment that their farming is a means to better stewardship of their time and money.

Derk says:

We're going to farm to the best of our ability, and make the most money we can in an ethical way. It's been more than twelve years since a border patrol came to our property. They gave up trying to find illegal aliens, because we would not hire them.

Why has this partnership worked so well when so many others fail?

John responds:

That's easy for me. From the very first time we started, our number one commitment was that we were stewards of that which God had given us. Secondly, we made a commitment to meet on a regular basis at least weekly to pray together, to plan, to discern the Lord's will in whatever we were doing.

Sometimes during the harvest, when they are too busy to meet in the office, the two partners meet out in the orchard to pray. "We don't try to go on vacation together, or play racquetball or whatever," Derk adds, "but we do a lot of talking together."

It's very clear that the bottom line of this partnership is not to make a lot of money but to glorify God with their lives through farming. But it comes as no surprise that they have become the largest peach growers for the biggest cooperative canning company in the world.

Just as Derk recognized his need for a partner if he was going to be a successful career farmer, so the need for partnership is emerging everywhere.

Partnering, A Guide to Co-Owning Anything from Homes to Home Computers,[1] describes ways in which people can partner in joint ownership. Author Lois Rosenthal says partnership saves money, shares work and avoids loneliness.

Cheri Fuller writes in *Focus on the Family,*[2] "Parents and teachers are partners in education, and if we are going to work for the best interests of our children, we need to know our partners." Additionally, businesses are beginning to form partnerships with schools to provide "hands on" job training for their employees.

Even dieters have learned that partnering in their ordeal can, literally, lighten the load. Nancy dieted at least twenty times, but each time she lost interest in the struggle . . . until her husband took an active role. He quit snacking in front of her. He went shopping with her to steer her away from the cookies. When she met her target for the week, he took her to the movies. They both enjoyed the results when she lost fifty-five pounds in time for their daughter's wedding.

In her book, *Partnership Diet Programs,* author Kelly Brownell says diet-partners must be easy to talk with, understanding, uncritical, interested and "there."

Partnership is also taking place on a grand scale. For example, political bridge developments in Europe are changing the very meaning of nationalism.

Partnership for Power
American travelers can already see a difference when they arrive in

Europe. Passport control lines are a lot faster for those who carry
the E.C.C. passport, a common document for the twelve countries
of the European Economic Community. By 1992 travellers will
have to go through only one passport control when entering Europe
and move around the other eleven countries without ever showing
their document again.

The European Economic Community will officially be inaugurat-
ed when the new trade and economic laws take effect in 1992. This
is not a political union but an economic partnership between independent nations to make Europe competitive with the fast-growing
economies of the Pacific Rim and with North America. Separately,
these European nations are no match for the Pacific Rim or North
America; but together the European Economic Community forms
the most powerful economy in the world. With free movement of
people, money and resources, trade barriers will be removed and
prices should come down.

Other European nations are clamoring to join the community.
Some think there may be at least eighteen countries in partnership
by the turn of the century. As in any partnership, members will
sacrifice some of their independence, and perhaps even their identity; but even cautious leaders like Margaret Thatcher are reluctant
to be left out of the resulting bonanza.

Partnering for a Better World
While power politics may feed the needs of greed more than solving
the problems of the poor, other partnerships around the world
target those who are least fortunate.

Most of us have seen a picture of former President Jimmy Carter
wearing a red cap on his head and a carpenter's apron tied around
his waist, helping to build a home for a family without decent
shelter. Habitat for Humanity partners with destitute families to
provide affordable housing with interest-free loans.

Habitat was founded by Millard Fuller, a self-made millionaire before the age of thirty, who realized his life was meaningless and empty. At Koinonia Farms, a Christian community in Americus, Georgia, Fuller and his wife made a commitment to share their Christian values by helping the poor get simple, decent homes. Many recipients had been living in tumble-down shacks without running water, paying higher rents than their new interest-free mortgage payments.

Habitat volunteers, like Jimmy Carter, build the buildings and the new owners take responsibility for repaying the privately funded loans. Habitat chooses not to accept federal funding. "We do not want to compromise our ability to proclaim that [Christian] message," maintains Fuller.

The new homeowners themselves are expected to put about 500 hours of "sweat equity" into the project in one form or another. Through such partnerships, Habitat has built more than 5,000 homes since 1976.

While Habitat provides interest-free loans to home buyers, other development agencies depend on interest return from their loans to generate new funds for other recipients.

CBS's "60 Minutes" focused a moving segment on the Grameen Bank in Bangladesh, a grassroots banking method enabling the poorest of the poor (earning thirty-five cents a day) to develop a life-sustaining business with loans as small as six dollars. The 16% interest rate supports the field bankers who go from village to village to collect the loans, and the profits return to the stockholders, 75% of whom are small Bengali business people.

A Christian organization, OPPORTUNITY International, based in Oak Brook, Illinois, forms partnerships with boards of Christian businesspeople in the Two-Thirds World.* OPPORTUNITY not only

---

*The term *Two-Thirds World* generally refers to the same countries as the term *Third World* but more accurately suggests the proportion of the world's population and land mass represented by these nations.

makes grants to its partner-agencies, but provides training in business management, accounting and cost-effectiveness. The partner-agency makes loans, averaging $1,000, to entrepreneurs to expand their small businesses and provide jobs for others. OPPORTUNITY estimates that one job is created for every $500 loan.

After five years the grants cease, and it is expected that returns on loans will form a growing, revolving fund. In twenty years loan repayments have averaged 90 per cent. In a single year OPPORTUNITY's partners created over 9,000 new jobs. For example, Paul is a Jamaican potter earning about $2,000 a year, laboriously shaping clay pots by hand. ASSIST (OPPORTUNITY's partner-agency in Jamaica) lent Paul $800 to purchase a flywheel and asked Jamaica's leading potter to train him to use it. In just one year Paul doubled his production and even hired another person to work for him.

Partnering for Survival

Multinational companies have long been a part of the international business world. But in contrast to these monoliths which decide policies and products for each branch, partnerships between autonomous companies are becoming more common.

Voicing the fears of many in the industrial world, the vice president of Chrysler Corporation warned that the automobile industry will not survive in the next decade without global alliances or partnerships. Our global interdependence, competitiveness, lack or abundance of resources and the rising power of nations in the Two-Thirds World will increasingly demand that we work together if we are going to achieve our goals.

"American companies once rode into alien countries as fearlessly as the Lone Ranger without Tonto," wrote Louis Kroar in his article,"Your Rivals Can Be Your Allies."[3] "Now they enlist a partner who knows his way around the local gullies." Over a ten-year period, 57 per cent of corporate partnerships did not work out. The pitfalls derive less from economics than relationships. "Executives . . . talk about alliances in terms ordinarily used to describe marriages, such as compatibility and trust," says Kroar.

The major tension in recent years has been finding a trade niche with Japan. The only way to ease that tension, according to the vice president of Motorola, is to "partner up."

IBM and six competitors did just that, forming a joint venture to manufacture and sell dynamic, random-access memory chips (DRAM). But in January 1990 the new consortium, U. S. Memories, was abandoned before it had even really started. Industry analysts said lack of support from other major electronics companies made it impossible to go ahead with what would have been the first manufacturing project of its kind in U.S. corporate history.

Partners for Love and Money

There is no form of partnership under greater attack than marriage. Fifty per cent of American marriages end in divorce today. Husbands and wives either don't recognize what the essential requirements of a good marriage partnership are, or they are unwilling to make a meaningful commitment. When partners don't share the same goals, the relationship is doomed to failure. An old Chinese proverb puts it simply, "Same bed; different dreams."

So warped are our expectations of marriage that TV producers have decided wholesome family sitcoms like "The Cosby Show" are too unrealistic for most viewers. Evidently audiences find it easier to identify with "Roseanne" or "Married with Children."

Yet many couples not only succeed as marriage partners but have the courage to become business partners as well. At least one million couples in the U.S.A. are in business together. To succeed each one contributes his or her unique skills to the relationship without a spirit of competition between them. They know how to handle conflict, accept objective criticism, avoid blame to the other for failure and rejoice in each other's success as a mutual benefit. They trust and respect each other. Just as John and Derk have done, they have to be able to divide responsibilities according to each other's strengths and weaknesses, and they talk together a lot.

Meet the Briscoes

Stuart and Jill Briscoe are such business partners. Stuart has been pastor of the Elmbrook Church in the suburbs of Milwaukee since 1970. His powerful, practical preaching, his British humor and his charismatic personality have made him one of the most popular speakers and Bible teachers at conferences across the country and around the world. He preaches to over six thousand people at Elmbrook every Sunday that he's there.

Stuart's equally gifted wife, Jill, is a powerful speaker and Bible teacher in her own right. With a style that is down-to-earth, witty and disarmingly honest, she has brought the Lord Jesus Christ closer and made him dearer to countless men, women and children throughout the world. The author remembers a mission conference some years ago when Stuart was to speak to all the gathered missionaries. Relaxed and casual in an old blue sweater, he stood up, introduced his wife and said that he felt she had a more pertinent message for us that morning.

The Briscoes are both prolific writers, having published dozens of books in the past twenty years. They are also the founders of "Telling the Truth," a non-profit audiocassette ministry of Bible teaching and practical discipleship. Their messages are heard on Christian radio stations around the world, and their tapes are sold wherever they speak and through direct mail.

While sharing their common goal to give clarity and understanding to the Word of God, they are often separated as they fulfill their various ministries. Jill admits that they are very independent of each other. "For example," she recalls, "Stuart has never even asked my opinion about what invitations he takes. I ask his secretary where he is, which I've done for years."

At the same time he encourages her to fulfill the mission God has called her to. "He's thanked me many times for letting him . . . go where he's wanted to go. . . . When I started to travel, which wasn't until I was over here, he's tried to do the same for me," Jill comments.

But while they retain their individuality and use their unique gifts for God's glory, they are in reality a very close partnership, often sharing the platform at conferences or travelling to mission fields to serve together.

In a very special way Stuart and Jill demonstrate the power of the "three-stranded cord." Bound together by the love of Christ and the guidance of the Holy Spirit, they are demonstrating a partnership of infinite strength, "a cord of three strands [which] is not quickly broken."

Chapter 2

Partnering Goes Back a Long Way

T he Christian faith is replete with models of partnership. When God said, "Let us make man in our image," he gave us a glimpse of the divine cooperative purposes of the Trinity right from the time of creation.

Our partnership with Christ is a fellowship which demonstrates his life and reality to a watching world. He strengthens us and gives us spiritual gifts so that we are better able to serve him (1 Cor 1: 5-9).

With all its teaching on individual responsibility for personal salvation and growth, Christianity stresses far broader relationships. The body is made up of many interrelated parts; the concerns for "each other's welfare," the beautifying of the bride in preparation for the celebration of the marriage feast with the groom. All speak of a unity of many for the glory of one.

New Testament Partnerships

In the New Testament Paul depended on his partners in ministry to accomplish his work for God. The Antioch church sent him on his first missionary journey as part of a three-man team: Barnabas, John Mark and Paul.

Both Paul and Barnabas had been teaching in Antioch for several years, and the church recognized their missionary gifts. As an apostle and eyewitness of the life of Jesus, John Mark brought tremendous credibility to their ministry. But for reasons unknown, John Mark left the team in Pamphylia.

John Mark's decision proved the undoing of the very first missionary team. Barnabas, older, and possibly wiser and more forgiving, wanted to give the younger man a second chance. But goal-oriented Paul didn't want to be encumbered with someone who had proven himself undependable. The disagreement intensified until the team broke up, Barnabas and John Mark going to Cyprus (where we lose touch with Barnabas in Scripture) and Paul choosing another partner in Silas. Though the partnership failed, Scripture does not record which, if any, of the partners was in the wrong.

The Philippian Partnership

Paul and Silas headed north, back into modern Turkey, with evidently no intentions of going on into Europe. But the "Macedonian call" changed their itinerary, and, as a result, Paul developed one of the sweetest and most effective partnerships of his ministry.

Philippi, the leading city of Macedonia, came under the rule of a Roman proconsul, giving the people the protection and rights of Roman citizens. Nevertheless, Paul later described the Macedonian churches as suffering "extreme poverty" (2 Cor 8:2).

As was his usual custom when arriving at a new city, Paul looked for a Jewish synagogue, but instead simply found a group of women praying by the river. One of them, Lydia, a businesswoman from Thyatira, was a devout seeker after God. She became Paul's first convert in Philippi, followed by the jailer and his family after Paul's miraculous release from prison, and a slave girl who'd been a fortuneteller.

Paul was able to return to visit Philippi at least twice on his journeys. The church, which by the time of the Philippian letter was large enough to have elders and deacons, developed a close, caring relationship with Paul. Though he loved all the churches dearly and prayed for them constantly, the Philippian church held a special place in his heart in spite of the insulting way he was treated in the city on his first visit. (How deeply his unfair jailing affected him can be seen by his reference to it in his letter to the Thessalonians [1 Thess 2:2]).

Missiologist George Peters describes this partnership in the following way:

> Paul's partnership relationship was one of full participation in the life of the churches and in their mobilization and enlistment in prayer, personnel and finances in evangelism. Paul discovered the resources for all his advances in evangelism and church expansion in the churches he planted. Thus the churches became involved with Paul from the very beginning in an aggressive program of evangelism and church multiplication. . . . It was a total partnership ministry from the very beginning.[1]

Ingredients of a Philippian Partnership

Paul expressed his special love for the Philippians when he wrote to them, "I thank my God every time I remember you. In all my prayers for all of you, I always pray with joy because of your partnership in the gospel" (Phil 1:3-5). What a beautiful way for a missionary to write to his supporting church.

The Greek word *koinonia,* used for partnership in Philippians, can also be translated as "fellowship." Lightfoot comments that this is far more than a friendly atmosphere in a public meeting. In Greek secular usage the word referred to marriage contracts and business relationships, agreements that involved sharing of privileges and responsibilities.

Paul and the Philippian Christians have been working together in partnership for possibly ten to twelve years (if Paul's imprisonment in Rome is the acceptable date of writing the letter). They have gone to great efforts to communicate with each other, even sending emissaries back and forth over long treacherous miles, and the church has, out of its poverty, sent gifts for Paul's ministry. They have been constantly in each other's prayers as both have worked to "advance the gospel." The partnership has been a deep source of joy to both, a "sacred fellowship," bound together in their common love for Christ and urgency to make him known.

What are the ingredients of this Philippian partnership? Are there qualities that should be part of our partnerships, whether they be between individuals, churches or missions? In this chapter we'll analyze the Paul/Philippian partnership, and in the next chapter we'll look at ingredients of successful partnerships for the twenty-first century. There are some significant similarities.

Partnering in the Gospel

A unique partnership formed between Paul the missionary and the believers who fellowshipped together in Philippi. Paul rejoices in partnership but not simply because he loves the believers and has enjoyed their care and concern for him personally. He expresses his joy because they have partnered together in the Gospel.

He's excited to report to them that, even though he's in prison, he's able to tell people about Christ, so that "the whole palace guard" knows why he's there. And because of the unique prison arrangements of those days, many have heard from his own lips about the Savior King. He wants them to know that their prayers and concern have helped him reach their common goal.

In turn, he's sending Timothy to them. He's no doubt given him a lot of verbal instructions and exhortations for them, but he also wants to find out all the news from Philippi. He may have been interested in who had gotten married, who's had a baby and who's found a new job. But he especially wants to know about their progress in the gospel: How are they doing in preaching the good news? That is the common goal that binds them together and keeps the partnership working.

Paul keeps reaching out farther and farther, possibly eventually to Spain, and exposing himself to greater dangers in order to make Christ known. And he expresses his concern that he could lose his life in the process. He's not afraid of death, but he realizes that by staying alive he can still contribute a lot to the growth and development of the Philippians so they can more perfectly share Christ as they "progress . . . in the faith" (Phil 1:25).

Watching a partner progress in faith is a great source of joy. Partners International, previously known as Christian Nationals Evangelism Commission (CNEC), is an organization that exists to participate with Christian ministries around the world to fulfill the Great Commission. After the Communists took over China, Partners International began helping ministries in Singapore. Schools, churches and other programs were established. Today most of these are financially independent, but we still continue to partner financially with some of these Southeast Asian ministries. Why? Because we share the same goal: to make Christ known in Southeast Asia. They keep stretching themselves, sending short-termers into Thailand, planting churches in tribal villages, opening up new work in Burma. Without their vision and zeal, our outreach into Southeast Asia would be very limited. Without our supplementary help, their outreach would be limited. But we rejoice in the privilege to partner "in the Gospel" together.

Partnering in the Spirit

As Paul begins to deal with some of the problems he's heard about in Philippi, he reminds them in Philippians 2:1 that their fellowship in the Spirit is their source of victory. Partnership in the Spirit can be represented by the "third strand" in a cord that is not easily broken. The Holy Spirit indwells all of them, and therefore is available for guidance, strength, wisdom and comfort. The Holy Spirit helps them make right decisions and purifies relationships. In letters to other churches, Paul spends a great deal of time explaining how to walk in the Spirit and to develop the fruits of the Spirit. In order to experience the blessings of the Spirit in this partnership, he urges them to submit themselves to the Spirit's control so that his joy would be complete.

Paul assumed that all members of the partnership could enjoy the benefits of the Spirit's influence. On the other hand, walking in the Spirit is a conscious effort that both Paul and the Philippians had to practice daily to maintain an intimate relationship and an effective ministry.

Unity in Partnership

No partnership is perfect, and every partnership faces some kind of testing. Though Paul did not deal with a major sin in the Philippian church as he did in Corinth, or a serious doctrinal issue as in Galatia, he intimated there were some areas that could cause problems. "Make my joy complete by being like-minded, having the same love, being one in spirit and purpose" (Phil 2:2).

Epaphroditus had evidently brought disturbing news of disunity in the body. It might even have had to do with Paul, for he speaks of those who "preach Christ out of selfish ambition . . . supposing that they can stir up trouble for me" (1:17). The fact that he wrote about this to the Philippians would indicate these people were either from Philippi or had passed through and were known to them.

Gently, tenderly, as a person coming alongside a close friend, he enjoins, ". . . make my joy complete by being like-minded, having the same love, being one in spirit and purpose" (2:2). Paul did not take sides in the issue (as he had to do in the case of immorality in Corinth) but encouraged unity in spirit and purpose.

There must have been a tremendous respect for each other's integrity for Paul to be able to counsel them in this way. A partnership that has built a strong relationship, as Paul and the Philippians had, can weather the problems that are bound to arise.

Partners Help Each Other to Grow

Each partner in the Philippian relationship wanted the other to grow, to give the other the opportunity, capacity or means to fulfill his mission. This key element of partnership is reflected over and over in the letter (Phil 2:4-8; 3:20; 4:21).

When Paul introduces himself to his partner church in Philippi, he does not use his normal identification tag. In the rest of his letters, with two exceptions, he identifies himself as Paul the apostle, conveying the idea of his authority. To the Philippian partners he chooses to identify as a servant . . . a servant of Christ coming to be a servant of the Christians in Philippi.

He also plans to send Timothy to them, to encourage them and enable them to resolve some of their personal difficulties. Paul knows of no one else who will take such a genuine interest in their welfare (2:19-20). He has served with Paul as a slave of Christ and has proven his value as one who knows how to enable others to grow.

Above all, Paul points to the supreme example of Christ who gave himself completely to enable us to become like him (3:21). Paul describes Jesus, the model servant, as the enabler par excellence. From this model, we can draw out some principles of enablement which apply to a healthy Christian partnership:

1. Look out for your own interests so that you will grow, but also look out for the interests of your partner (2:4).

2. Develop a servant attitude (2:5-9).

3. Continually give of yourself to meet the legitimate needs of your partner (2:8).

4. Identify with your partner (2:7).

5. Recognize that enablement is costly. You may have to renounce some of your own rights (2:8).

When the Nigerian EMS (Evangelical Mission Society) missionaries came into contact with the Maguzawa tribe in northern Nigeria, they were astounded to learn that these people were open to the gospel. Rather than being staunch Muslims as the predominant tribes around them, their name actually meant "runners from Islam," for they had refused over the centuries to accept Muslim teaching.

Now they begged the EMS missionaries to send workers to teach them about Jesus Christ. But where would the missionaries come from to take advantage of this ripe opportunity?

The mission approached Simon Ibraham, then general secretary of the Evangelical Church of West Africa (ECWA) church, to ask for help. When the opportunity was presented at the annual church conference, God's Spirit moved upon many of the older pastors as well as the graduates of the Bible school. Initially sixteen pastors offered to give up their churches and move their families into the Maguzawa field. Not only did the Nigerian missionaries make great personal sacrifices to open up this new work, but the churches willingly gave up their pastors. The ECWA church enabled EMS to enter a new field with a timely bold thrust which resulted in 200 Maguzawa churches being planted in just five years.

Partnership in Suffering

Paul wanted to know the fellowship of suffering with Christ (Phil 3:10). He was willing to pay whatever price was required to know and serve Christ fully. And he knew as he suffered, Christ would not forsake him.

While Paul could not add to the work of atonement, R. Martin in his commentary states:

. . . we must not evacuate the phrase of its rich meaning by taking it to mean simply that he shared his Lord's sufferings in imagination or sympathy.

Beaten or imprisoned, shipwrecked or shackled, Paul gladly suffered for Christ's sake knowing his Savior had gone through much deeper suffering for him. Every pain helped him to better know and identify with Christ's pains endured for him.

Often, suffering for Christ is a lonely road, and nothing can be gained by simply volunteering to suffer with another for suffering's sake. Yet when we can fellowship in suffering by helping to alleviate the intensity or supplying encouragement and fortitude in the pain, it is part of our commitment as partners.

A Christian wife watched her husband dying from painful pancreatic cancer. Caring for him was difficult, but she knew that he wanted to stay at home with family and familiar things around him, rather than go to the sterile environment of the hospital. Night after night, she continued to sleep beside him, holding him in his pain, crying with him, suffering with him. Many times she told him, "I wish I could bear the pain for you." Until the partnership ended, she fellowshipped in his suffering as part of her identity with the one she loved.

Financial Partnership

To most people partnership implies funding, usually the "have's" funding the "have nots." Even in this first-century partnership, money played a key role.

Both Paul and the Philippians would be considered "have nots." Paul described the Macedonia churches, like Philippi, as being in "extreme poverty." Though he never asked for money for himself, he thanked them profusely for their gifts explaining, "You sent me aid again and again when I was in need" (Phil 4:16).

The Philippians seemed to have learned financial partnering right from the early days of their relationship with Paul. Their financial obligation was frosted with love and concern, as they sent their gifts with Epaphroditus so he could help in other ways and report back the situation in which he found Paul.

Other churches took longer to learn their financial responsibilities, for Paul rather sadly confessed that besides the Philippians "not one church shared with me in the matter of giving" (4:15).

While Paul did not ask for funds for his own personal needs (in fact he tried to support himself with his tent-making skills whenever he could) he did not hesitate to "fund-raise" for others. His dramatic appeal to the Corinthians used the Macedonian churches as examples of generous giving out of poverty. He even dared make comparisons (4:15-18), stating candidly that their giving was an indication of their love.

He appealed to the wealthy Corinthians on the basis of how much they had so that they would share with the Jerusalem Christians who were in dire need at the time. Giving often is part of a chain reaction. Paul's Philippian partners sent funds to him for his needs as well as for others. In turn, Paul urged wealthy Corinthians to give to Jerusalem Christians. Each gift resulted in thanksgiving to God and became an act of joyful fellowship.

The Korean church has learned to give generously and creatively. For some years Partners International has partnered with Operation Lighthouse, a church-planting ministry in rural Korea where 33 per cent of the people are Buddhists. Most of the nation's accelerating church growth has taken place in the urban areas, and along with growth has come a burgeoning interest in world missions. But though Korean churches helped support their own rural church planters, they were limited in funding missionaries around the world because they could not transfer money out of the country.

A three-way partnership developed which released prayer and a far-reaching missions commitment. North American sponsors formed a partnership with rural Korean church-planters and sent assistance through Partners International. The Korean urban churches selected a number of missionaries in places such as Africa or India for prayer and financial involvement. Instead of sending funds to Korea, money was transferred to their missionaries in other parts of the world, while Korean churches sent an equal amount of money to Operation Lighthouse.

As Two-Thirds World missions continue to grow, we will see an increasing variety of creative financial partnerships develop, with their roots right in the Pauline letters.

Prayer Partnership

The intimacy of this special partnership is nowhere better reflected than in Paul's closing words, "Therefore, my brothers, you whom I love and long for, my joy and crown, . . . dear friends" (4:1).

How was this intimacy maintained? How did they express their concern for one another? Prayer was the cement that bonded them in love; prayer was the power that held the structure together; prayer was the framework that gave the partnership shape; prayer released the Holy Spirit's work in each of them.

Paul's warmth of love and emotion pours itself out in fervent, frequent prayers of praise for what this partnership has meant to him (Phil 1:3-4, 9, 19; 4:16). What must it have been like to listen in on those prayers of boundless joy as he brought this precious body before the Lord?

No doubt he prayed for health, for safety and protection, for families and relationships. He must have longed for such personal news and must have plied Epaphroditus with dozens of questions when he arrived with their gift. Now he was planning to send Timothy to them for more information. Effectual prayer thrives on communication.

But Paul's prayers for his partners plumbed far greater depths than their personal health and welfare. He prayed that they would love more, learn more about spiritual truth, and gain discernment to make the right choices in their constant upward walk. Anticipating the time when their physical partnership would end, he taught them "in everything, by prayer and petition, with thanksgiving, present your requests to God" (4:6). Though for now, his enablement was so important for their growth that he preferred to stay in this life rather than go to be with Christ. He wanted them to be ready to trust that God alone could indeed "supply all their needs."

But as in all good partnerships, the benefits flow in two directions, and Paul assured the Philippians that their prayers had been a great help and encouragement to him, and that he believed they would effect his "deliverance."

When we realize that Paul and the Philippians probably only met face to face three times over ten or twelve years, that their communications were limited to an occasional letter carried by hand over treacherous land and sea and a rare visit from a mutual friend, we know that the bonding between them came from the Holy Spirit himself. Eighteen centuries later, John Fawcett captured the ethos of this relationship in these words:

Blest be the tie that binds
Our hearts in Christian love;
The fellowship of kindred minds
Is like to that above.

Before our Father's throne
We pour our ardent prayers;
Our fears, our hopes, our aims are one,
Our comforts and our cares.

We share each other's woes,
Each other's burdens bear;
And often for each other flows
The sympathizing tear.

But while we recognize the beauty of the first-century partnership between Paul and the Philippians, we wonder if such a partnership can work in the twenty-first century. Are there other ingredients necessary to maintain a working partnership? Do the problems of our fast-paced technological society demand more of partners to make the relationship work today?

Chapter 3

From Paternalism to Partnership

C harles and June Foster took turns all night bathing the burning body of their young son. Edgar had been screaming and thrashing in pain for several days until in desperation they sent an African messenger for the doctor, three hundred miles away by bicycle. But now Edgar simply stared dully at them, his body limp and quiet, the silence more ominous than his cries.

By the time the African messenger returned with a note from Dr. Fisher that he could not leave his patients to make the long trek, six-month old Mabel had also contracted the mysterious illness and died. Edgar survived; his body continued to grow, but his mind had quit functioning. Later medical evaluations pointed to meningitis, but there was no cure for the disease in 1922. For years June would lovingly care for her son, who physically grew to be a man, but whose mouth never uttered her name and whose eyes never lit in a smile when she walked into the room. Eventually, to protect their children's health, the Fosters left all four others in Canada, separated from them for seven or eight years at a time, while they returned to serve the Lord among the unreached Bakaonde in northern Rhodesia (now Zambia.)

Pioneer missionaries like the Fosters went to the remote corners of the world, knowing disease, suffering and early death were inevitable. Many packed their outgoing gear into coffins which they took with them.

For example, in 1817 John Williams was killed and eaten by cannibals in the South Seas Islands. In 1826 Adoniram Judson's wife, Ann, died of fever in Burma, followed just a few weeks later by her infant daughter, Marie. In 1900, 200 missionaries were killed in the Boxer Rebellion in China. In West Africa 19 out of 20 Western missionaries died of tropical diseases within two years after their arrival. The gospel of Jesus Christ was brought to the far-flung corners of the world at great personal sacrifice by these pioneer missionaries. Yet they continued to go to share Christ with primitive people who had never seen a White man before, who could not read or write and who looked upon these messengers of God as gods themselves.

Colonial Influence

In India, Africa and other parts of the world Europeans colonized the land and brought certain amenities and Western comforts with them. Though missionaries did not come as political emissaries, it is understandable that they found the presence and protection of the colonial representatives comforting. And unfortunately, it was all too easy to slip into colonial relationships with the simple, unsophisticated and uneducated heathen they had come to reach.

Seldom did a native evangelist enter through the missionary's front door; never did he sit in his living room or eat off his dishes. Even when he was given opportunities to teach or lead a congregation, it was under the guidance and control of the missionary, who paid his salary and controlled his destiny.

Missiologist R. Pierce Beaver wrote, " . . . all missionaries were colonialistic and paternalistic to the end of the 19th century." Mission leaders believed, for example, that Africans were inferior and could not produce leadership for the church.

Missionaries in China, while faithfully putting down the roots of the church which has flourished so astoundingly during the communist oppression, miscalculated the rich cultural heritage of China's long history. Missionaries carefully packed their "china" to take with them, unaware that the very process of making porcelain had been developed in China centuries earlier.

Christianity became synonymous with the West's condescension. A strong yearning to be free from such Western patronage and disdain contributed to the desire of China's political leaders to find an answer for China. The Russian Revolution sparked hope, and a young leader from the hinterland of China emerged: Mao Tsetung. Mao led the communist forces to victory in 1949 and declared, "Our nation will never again be an insulted nation."

Like many parents, missionaries believed that they needed to protect their "children," think for them and guide them into maturity. According to Ralph Winter, this first era of paternalism lasted well into the twentieth century. Unfortunately, remnants of such paternalism still exist.

The concept of independence and partnership developed gradually. At the Edinburgh Missions Conference in 1910, only 17 national leaders attended (out of 1300 delegates), and the national church's dissatisfaction with the older structure surfaced. Bishop Azariah of India pled eloquently with the missions, "Give us friends." But, at the 1947 conference 37 years later, even though mission leaders talked about "partnership in obedience," much of it still remained lip service.

Political Pressures Force Independence

Other forces, however, were moving the national churches toward independence. During the Second World War, many missionaries left the fields, and the churches were thrust into making their own decisions and developing their own leadership. With the war's end came political independence for a large number of countries, and the national church believed its time for independence had come as well.

The era of nationalism was traumatic as the national churches flexed their independence muscles, and church-mission tensions became the top order of discussion at every gathering of missionaries. It was as though their "child" had become a "rebellious teen-ager," and they were confused about how to handle the problem.

Even greater shocks were to come when in 1971 African leader John Gatu called for a moratorium of missionaries. The cry of "missionary go home" was not heard broadly, but it stirred missions everywhere to rethink their strategies. They began to wonder what had gone wrong.

Obstacles to Partnership

From hindsight it seems simple to say missions and national churches should have thought about forming equal partnerships long ago. Third-World Christian leaders ask why has it taken us so long? Why do we lack the patience and faith to partner with them? Why are we unwilling to risk by allowing them to make their own mistakes? Many obstacles to true partnership have slowed the process.

1. *Western missions have had to work through their own ethnocentricity.*

The belief that "West is best" blinded us to the values found in other cultures and to the realization that the truth of Scripture can be adapted to each culture, allowing each people to develop its own forms of worship and lifestyle. Appreciation of the beauty of God-given diversity in other cultures, and especially in the church, was difficult.

Some early missions even segregated new believers from the rest of society in order to purify them. In the seventeenth century Cotton Mather encouraged the establishment of Christian towns among the North American Indians. He believed segregation and isolation necessary to a convert's growth to "ensure a more decent and English way of living."

Missions have come a long way since then in accepting and strengthening the good aspects in other cultures in which they are sharing the gospel and allowing the church to flourish naturally in the cultural soil.

2. *The overpowering resources of the West developed a donor mentality.*

Missiologist Walbert Buhlmann says this Western donor attitude makes the Third World church "a kindergarten for Mother Church and a poorhouse for the exercise of her charity."[1] Western churches have been guilty of showering money and personnel on the national churches without thinking through the potentially negative results.

For example, a young African missionary spoke in American churches, presenting the church-planting ministry of his denomination in an unreached area of his country. He vividly described the difficulties of travel—walking, or riding a bicycle for many miles under the burning sun. Christians listened sympathetically and responded impulsively, offering to purchase a motorcycle for him.

However, these generous donors had not taken the time to find out that the young missionary's older colleague back on the field walked just as far and with more difficulty because of health problems. He had asked the church leaders for transportation, and they were trying to find ways to fund his request. It's easy to understand the resentment and bitterness he felt when his junior, who'd been selected to go to the United States because of his fluency in English, had come back with a motorcycle.

The unthinking donors had not only unwittingly caused jealousy between workers, but usurped the church's role in making decisions about its missionaries' requests. Partnership would have avoided such pitfalls, but the mentality to give emotionally and personally often bypasses partnership agreements.

3. *The Two-Thirds World church became a prisoner of history.*

Though Two-Thirds World church leaders recognized how the controls and the resource power of the West had weakened the church, many could not let go, afraid to give up the security of outside funding.

David Bosch, professor of missiology at the University of South Africa, draws an analogy from African farmers who set traps to catch baboons who are destroying their crops. They cut a hole in the top of a pumpkin just large enough for the baboon's hand to squeeze in. The baboon reaches in to get the delicious seeds, but is unable to get his clenched fist back out through the hole. It sits there helplessly, a prisoner of the pumpkin until the farmer comes to shoot it. It never realizes that all it has to do is to let go of the seeds!

In order to keep the money and free mission personnel, national churches publicly accepted the dominance and control of the West, while in their own circles hotly complaining about paternalism.

4. *The "three-self" theory of missions hindered the development of partnership.*

There's no doubt that the concepts of self-support, self-propagation and self-administration were necessary to enable national churches to become independent bodies, fully mature and acknowledging the Holy Spirit as the giver of all necessary gifts for growth and sustenance.

Nineteenth-century mission leaders propounded the theory as the goal of missions, to counteract the dominance of missions and the dependency of the national church. They feared that churches wouldn't develop as long as the Western missionaries were around. They believed that the national Christians would neither give nor trust God to supply their needs locally, as long as they could rely on Western funding. Overreacting, they failed to apply the biblical principles of "giving to those in need" to the conditions in the Third World.

Mission organizations instituted cutbacks on funding for pastors so that, over a certain period of time, the church would be fully responsible for the pastor's salary. What funds were sent to the fields remained in the control of the missionaries, to be spent at their discretion so as not to "spoil" the local Christians.

The period of withdrawing personnel and funds from local churches was perhaps necessary in order to give the churches freedom to become independent and mature. But unfortunately it also separated the older and younger churches. Some national leaders found it difficult to work together side by side on the same field with well-funded Western missionaries. To the nationals, the Western agency seemed to have all the money and personnel it needed to start new programs which it could run with its own personnel and funds, rather than coming alongside the younger churches it had brought into being.

With the new era of partnership, the pendulum is swinging back, not to paternalism and dependency, but to helping each other fulfill the Great Commission.

5. *Partnership on a broad scale has been handicapped by disunity in the Christian world.*

In the late sixties a remarkable demonstration of partnership developed in West Africa. The first graduate-level seminary for French-speaking Africa was established through the cooperation of several Western missions and became the only graduate seminary for churches in all of French-speaking Africa (over 200 million people!). But the devil knew just how to defeat such a victory. Lecturers, trained in several leading evangelical American seminaries, taught from different theological perspectives. The administration, the students and the churches divided into two different camps, and the seminary nearly closed its doors.

Disunity in the church has been with us since some said, "I am of Paul and others, I am of Apollos," in the New Testament Church.

An Arab Christian asked for prayer for the tiny house church which met in his home in a North African country. In the entire city of several million Muslims, the seven families in the church were the only known Christians. Then one brother travelled to Europe on business and returned greatly blessed from fellowship with a charismatic church. He began to insist that others experience the same gifts he'd received, and a church-split resulted. Now there are two churches in this Muslim city: one of three families, the other four.

Rather than seeing that Christians are one body, as Jesus prayed, within the world we more often see such evidences of disunity as weakness and hypocrisy. When Evangelist Guy Sottile began his evangelistic ministry, Italy for Christ, in his native land, he urged pastors and churches of different denominations to work cooperatively with him to evangelize their cities and towns. For the first time these Protestant leaders have put aside their differences and worked together as a visible force, rather than being intimidated by their minority position in the country. God has blessed this unity with a tremendous response.

The rash of international conferences in the twentieth century have been a means of bringing together diverse sections of the church. At Lausanne II, the Congress on World Evangelism held in Manila in 1989, three obstacles to unity surfaced. Lyn Cryderman summarized them in the August 18, 1989, issue of *Christianity Today:* How will charismatics and non-charismatics work together? To what extent will social ministry characterize evangelical missions? And how will the predominantly middle-aged Western leadership of Lausanne respond to the growing prominence of a young Third-World church?

The Lausanne organization itself struggles with questions of

unity with such other international movements as the World Evangelical Fellowship and the A.D. 2000 Movement.

6. *Both Western and non-Western churches have been slow to*
understand each other's heartbeat and reluctant to speak openly
and candidly.

Unfortunately, when they have spoken to each other, often a lot
of repressed bitterness has spilled out first. But the international
missions conferences that have been held periodically since 1910
have not only encouraged unity, but have given all sides a neutral
forum at which to speak, and those who have attended have found
that there are people of good will on both sides.

The Lausanne Covenant, which came out of the 1974 congress,
included a pivotal statement which points to the hope that the end
of the long road to partnership is in sight. Article Eight reads:

We rejoice that a new missionary era has dawned. The dominant
role of Western missions is fast disappearing. God is raising up
from the younger churches a new resource for world evangelization, and is thus demonstrating that the responsibility to evangelize belongs to the whole body of Christ.

By 1980 at the Pattaya conference in Thailand, national Christian
leaders were predominant in preparation and participation, and
that conference became the great turning point for partnership in
missions.

The excitement is that we are on the doorstep of the greatest
mobilization in the history of the church. It's happening in every
country and every group of people. There's potential of greater
mobilization among women, young people, laypeople. Intergenerational partnership is emerging, with young leaders respecting the
wisdom and experience of the older; and older leaders rejoicing in
the creative leadership of younger leaders.

Charismatics and non-charismatics are working together for
world evangelization. And the Two-Thirds World and Western
Christians are developing mature relationships as partners too.

Dr. Tokunboh Adeyemo, general secretary of the Association of Evangelicals of Africa and Madagascar, stresses, "No single group—regardless of how skilled, gifted, experienced, or rich—can finish the task of world evangelization alone. It will take all the true Christian Church and para-church organizations all over the world working together in obedience to Christ."

Today, after many years of "talking," partnership mission leaders around the world are making tangible efforts to partner with the church in the Two-Thirds World. But partnership is complex at best and demands wisdom and effort to make it work. We'll look at the ingredients of successful partnerships in the chapters ahead.

Chapter 4

It Sounds Like a Marriage

F lying to international destinations now has an added bonus. You can earn mileage points by flying on "international partners," foreign airlines which have joined hands with U.S.-based lines, then stay in "partner hotels" and utilize "partner car rentals."

It's good for everybody's business, and with the U.S. airlines advertising their partners' routes and getting passengers to switch to related lines, everybody wins. Partnership enhances the business of each partner and offers the customers better service and the incentive of free travel.

The airlines have looked for other lines that connect with their routes, lines that will help their customers, that want their business, and offer the same quality of service their U.S. patrons expect. These partnerships are developed through long negotiations and careful analysis of the benefits to both. How different from take-overs and mergers that swallow up other companies and have seriously cut back the number of major airlines in this country.

Just as secular organizations are realizing the benefits of partnerships, so are missions and churches. Tim Lewis of Frontier Missions says:

> If we're looking at reaching the unreached people of the world, no single organization, no matter how powerful, how muscular it might be, has the capacity to do what needs to be done without the help of other people.

In fact, the majority of mission leaders would agree with Lewis, but making it happen in a sustained way is very hard work. Some agencies who have tried partnering have become disillusioned. They've had high aspirations and then been disappointed or were taken advantage of in the name of partnership. They're not willing to take a risk again.

Partnership can be very complex and fraught with hidden "mines" that sometimes don't blow up before the participants are well into the partnership. For that reason many fear the consequences, which might mean giving up their freedom and control, or losing their identity in a joint venture.

Yet there are enough working partnerships in the business, development and mission arena that key ingredients for success can be identified. Getting involved in partnership holds certain risks, but refusing to partner, particularly with Two-Thirds World churches or agencies, may mark the end of our own effectiveness in the world. "If we do not have partnership in mission," warns David Fraser, a research associate for the Mission Training and Resource Center, "we are bound to have a poverty of mission in the future."[1]

Definition of Partnership
But what do we mean by partnership? Is it simply cooperation between people? Is it a pact to help each other accomplish a specific task?

Before looking at the ingredients for successful partnerships, it is important that we arrive at a working definition. Definitions will vary according to where the person is coming from. A Bengali development leader defined *partnership* as "bringing equal or nearly equal resources to bear on resolving the problems of poverty in the south [southern hemisphere]." This however, seems to be a one-sided definition, giving little opportunity for the south to contribute to the northern partner.

For a basic description, and open to review, we will define partnership in missions as an association of two or more autonomous bodies who have formed a trusting relationship and fulfill agreed-upon expectations by sharing complementary strengths and resources, to reach their mutual goal.

As we discuss the ingredients of successful partnerships, each aspect of this definition will become clearer. We will cover five of the ten ingredients in this chapter and five more in the next chapter.

Ingredients for Success
1. *Partners agree on doctrine and ethical behavior.*

Richard taught a Bible class in his local church. His job allowed him to study while working, and since he was an avid reader, he enjoyed digging up every nuance of Greek meanings and background information of the passage.

Unfortunately Richard became very dogmatic about many aspects of biblical application, and began feeling uncomfortable with the pastor's teaching and the church's position on a number of questions.

He sat down and made a list of ninety-nine doctrinal points which he felt were essential if he were to continue having fellowship in the church. Though the elders agreed with most of his points, in fact all the essential ones, there were certain areas of disagreement. So, armed with his list, Richard left the church to find one that preached "the truth." Not surprisingly, after a few years of fruitless searching, Richard is back, finally willing to admit that no church could meet all his requirements.

Some Christians have a very narrow circumference of truth, beyond which they cannot comfortably associate with people who differ with them. Others who hold the same basic evangelical truths are able to cooperate with those who differ in nonessentials.

Churches and denominations across Latin America became part of the COMIBAM (Congress on Missions in Ibero-America) movement which culminated in the historical continent-wide missions congress in São Paulo, Brazil, in November 1987. While 80 per cent of evangelicals in Latin America are charismatic, noncharismatics were essential partners in the process. Throughout the history of the church these two segments have generally not worked together. But in focusing on the great cause of mission education and mobilization, the Latin church came together from a broad doctrinal base. The continent had crossed over from being a "mission field" to a "mission force," and all evangelical Christians had great cause to celebrate.

It is essential that potential partners understand each other's doctrinal positions and believe that they, and their constituency, can work comfortably together without making issues out of differences.

2. *Partners share a common goal.*

COMIBAM's common goal was to enthuse pastors and church leaders for missions and to mobilize Christians to get involved in world evangelization. COMIBAM did not attempt to plan cooperative ministries or form mission agencies. Each national group would develop its own strategy, allowing for the many differences in background, doctrine and state of the church. COMIBAM met its goal because it was clear to all involved.

Partners who focus on a common objective, rather than on enhancing their individual programs, will be far more successful than those whose goals are not clear. Personnel and resources will be shared, not only for the benefit of the partners but to better meet the mutual goal. Neither partner will retain ownership of its resources, nor resent the resources the other has; but, rather, both will rejoice that they are available to meet the common objective.

This can be especially helpful in maintaining good relationships between a funding agency and its partner ministries. When the resources used to develop donors and new sources of funding are recognized as essential to meet the partners' common goal, they will be seen in proper perspective, rather than competing with the ministry's program needs. And perhaps donors will also begin to accept that fund-raising and administration are as necessary to reaching the common goal as literature and missionary salaries.

3. *Partners must develop an attitude of equality.*

To some, partnership resembles the famous "safari stew" which calls for equal parts of elephant and rabbit: one elephant and one rabbit.

Equal partnership seems impossible since the West with its resources of money, technology, personnel and training is represented by the elephant. How can a Third-World church or agency feel equal with such a behemoth for a partner?

Yet the cry for equality is repeated almost without exception whenever Third-World leaders are asked about partnership. Neither side seems to understand the true meaning of equality. The West considers itself as "having arrived" in relation to its "developing" partners. Two-Thirds World Christians feel inferior, with little to offer, or so they think.

The problem lies with our understanding of equality, which has little to do with size, amount of resources or power. Rather, equality has everything to do with attitudes, values and status. Unfortunately we place an extremely high value on tangibles like money, education and technology. But the Scripture places little value on these. In fact, rather than being a value, money becomes simply a tool at best and a temptation at worst.

Secular development organizations struggle with the concepts of value too. They have recognized that the understanding of what will work in a culture, for example, affects the success of a project even more than money, and the local people have that ability.

Flying low over the coast of Lake Turkana in northern Kenya, one sees flocks of pink flamingoes which add the only touch of color to the drab desert landscape. The grass huts of the Turkana blend into the terrain, and only the dark shapes of people moving along the desert trails give any evidence of life.

Then suddenly a factory looms out of the vastness, a mammoth steel gray structure surrounded by high chain-link fences. But closer observation reveals nothing else: no people, no vehicles, no activity. A well-meaning development agency spent thousands of dollars erecting a fish-processing plant on the shores of Lake Turkana to provide a livelihood for the nomadic Turkanas. But the people could have told them that the project was doomed to failure. During drought conditions, spawning grounds dry up, and there are few fish in the lake. And once the drought conditions end so that the people can move their cattle away from government wells, they return to their nomadic existence. Besides that, by the time the frozen fish were transported several hundred miles to Nairobi, the costs were so astronomical that no one could afford to buy them.

Ridiculous as this may sound, Christian organizations have been known to finance and promote projects just as unsuitable to the spiritual environment. Cultural wisdom and understanding is just one of the intangible values that give Third-World partners equal status with their Western counterparts.

Third-World Christian leaders want to be recognized as spiritual equals, not only before God but with their partners.

Through its extraordinary experiences of mighty prayer (Korea), suffering (Eastern Europe) and martyrdom (China), the church around the world has demonstrated spiritual maturity from which the Western church can learn and be blessed.

Partners desire to be recognized as equal in selfhood and potential for maturity in Christ. Each partner must see himself or herself as made in God's image for God's purpose. Partners in ministry, just as men and women, are equal before God while differing in nature and function.

An attitude of equality requires that partners respect each other, listen to each other, learn from each other and trust each other. A national leader complained to his partner agency in North America, "We listen; we follow. That's not partnership."

Unintentionally Western churches sometimes treat great national Christian leaders disrespectfully. Nationals participated in the missions conference of a large church. In their own countries these Christian leaders directed large seminaries, served as heads of denominations and spoke at international congresses. But they complained that the missions conference made a spectacle of them. Asked to appear in "native costume" (which they never wear at home), they were given only ten minutes to tell a dramatic or shocking story and to summarize the impact of their ministry.

While Western partners need to continue to develop respect for and acceptance of their Third-World partners, these partners must also grow in their respect and acceptance of Western values such as the need for careful reporting and regular accounting.

An attitude of equality is a two-way street and can only be achieved in conjunction with the following essential ingredient.

4. *Partnership avoids dominance of one over the other.*

Who makes the decisions?

Who draws up policies?

Who controls the resources?

These are the questions Two-Thirds World leaders are asking when evaluating partnerships. If the answer is the "donor or sending agency" then there is serious doubt that this is a viable partnership.

Of course, partnership has been a gradual development, and

where there has been a long history of relationships, roles have changed. Just as in a family, parents dominate during the early years of childhood, gradually releasing controls until the children achieve full maturity. And then one day they find themselves calling the children up on the phone to ask their advice about a decision they're facing in their work or about our finances. That's when they realize that their children are adults.

Unfortunately, mission history is replete with illustrations of agencies who feel their "child" is in a perpetual state of adolescence. When they did turn over churches and institutions, it was a painful wrenching experience instead of a joyful unleashing of them to develop their own capabilities.

Dominance encourages dependency . . . in children and in ministries. In Africa a missionary put up a church building for a growing congregation. A few years later, the mission superintendent visited the church and noticed that the roof was leaking badly. He didn't say anything, assuming that the elders were making plans to fix it. A year later he returned again to find the roof in an even worse state of disrepair. The missionary asked the church leaders, "Why don't you fix the roof?"

The rather shocking reply was, "You built it, you fix it."

Though this is a rare instance, it does illustrate how dependency robs people of opportunity to exercise their gifts and leads to apathy.

Joint decision making at the grassroots level can be fairly easily worked out. But who makes decisions, designs policy and determines funding at the board level becomes more complex.

If each organization in the partnership is autonomous, should representatives from each board serve on the other partner's board? Do donors' designations promote dominance by the funding board? What decisions must be considered by all partners, and what decisions should be handled independently?

These "sticky wickets" have no easy answers, and partners in the

West and Two-Thirds World have complaints and suggestions about how it's working in their partnerships. The tendency to dominate in Western agencies and the desire for total freedom from controls and restrictions on the part of Two-Thirds World partners need to be worked at continually. And this will only happen if there is open and frequent communication.

5. *Partnership requires open communication.*

In his book *Megatrends,* Naisbitt described the trends that were shaping the 1980s. He listed the change from an industrial society to an information society as number one. In *Megatrends 2000* he reiterates, "the growth in information has only quickened."

Living in an information age vitally affects partnerships which have virtually become "information exchanges." Without this exchange it will become more and more difficult to maintain partnerships.

Unfortunately the pace of information exchange has accelerated in the West, and while some urban Two-Thirds World ministries can provide this increased information, others are lagging sadly behind. In the West sending information is almost equivalent to "faxing it." But national leaders living in rural areas of their countries are often without telephone or even reliable postal service. In some cases, especially in Muslim countries, they dare not report on their ministries for fear the mail will be intercepted.

Added to these technical difficulties are the inherent differences in communications systems. International partners need great sensitivity in communicating crossculturally. The Chinese value of face-saving, the African circuitous route at arriving at an issue and the Western direct, confrontational type of communication can be on a collision course.

Since misunderstanding can so easily arise in crosscultural communication, it is essential that partners communicate frequently, freely and personally in order to avoid misunderstanding. It has been said that "misinformation thrives in a vacuum."

At Partners International's official international conference in 1987, partnership was discussed openly, revealing many misconceptions and unfulfilled expectations. We learned that actions we'd taken, such as appointing regional coordinators, were seen as unilateral decisions. National leaders felt they should have had a voice in implementing such a major policy.

At the same conference, we were able to share some of our frustrations because of lack of timely reports. We explained increasing demands for information from donors and supporting churches and the embarrassment we face when missions committees ask for information and the data in our files is more than six months old. We were able to tell them why this information is necessary and how it is used, not just to maintain our credibility, but to further our common goals.

These gatherings are costly in time and money, but they are invaluable in the nurturing of the partnership into a more effective relationship.

However, conferences cannot take the place of personal contact. When our mission was smaller, then President Allen Finley travelled frequently to the fields, spending time regularly with each ministry. He and his wife, Ruth, knew each national personally, and were able to express love and attention. If a new baby arrived in a national's home, Ruth wrote a warm card of welcome. When a national leader married, a little gift would be carried to them on the next trip overseas. Such attention becomes more difficult as the number of ministries and nationals increases.

We recognize the importance of personal contact, not only on the family level, but in order to communicate one to one and to keep the channels open. We still give international visits high priority but have not been able to get to all ministries as frequently as we'd like. On a recent visit to Nigeria by one of our staff, the leader of our partner ministry there expressed, "We've missed visits from headquarters."

When national leaders visit the international headquarters, they meet with everyone on the staff with whom they've been dealing over the years. This face-to-face communication makes it easier to share victories and frustrations in the partnership.

Sometimes our partner leaders will frankly discuss our operations and make suggestions—even about our fund-raising methods. Sharing these insights is part of partnership. "We share our hearts with each other, rather than just keeping quiet," said one leader.

One area of communication that is particularly sensitive is accountability. It is also one of the essential ingredients of partnership.

Chapter 5

Maintaining a Balance

D
r. Henry Brandt, Christian psychologist and writer, used to tell the story about his young teen-age daughter's reactions when he set strict regulations about the time she was to be in at night.

"You act like you don't trust me, Daddy," she wailed.

"Of course I don't, my dear," her wise father responded.

He explained that while he trusted *her,* he did not trust her immature emotional development to be able to withstand the temptations she might face, and he wanted to protect her until she was more mature.

The sixth essential ingredient for a successful partnership deals with the whole matter of trust.

6. *Partners demonstrate trust and accountability.*

Dr. Brandt's observations may be wise counsel for parents and teen-agers, but Two-Thirds World Christian leaders are not adolescents needing to be protected. They should be recognized as mature, godly men and women who have the same spiritual resources for righteous living and wise judgments as their Western counterparts. On the other hand, Two-Thirds World partners will have to be careful not to arbitrarily accuse Western agencies of covering up ulterior motives.

A trust relationship grows out of a properly formed partnership. The ingredients of confidence are built into the initial understanding of each other's potential and agreements of what each expects of the other. In almost all the models of partnership we'll be looking at later in this book, partner organizations have drawn up written agreements and guidelines.

Careful partner selection is critical. There must be a sense of God's direction and a conviction that the Holy Spirit is leading both parties into the relationship. Boards, goals and objectives, administrative structures and financial policies should be analyzed by each partner. Obligations to each other have to be clearly spelled out so there is no misunderstanding later.

Several years ago, a Western and Third-World ministry were considering a partnership in Peru. However, as the Peruvian leaders studied what would be expected of them, they decided they would not be comfortable in the partnership and withdrew their application. Such careful analysis during the selection process avoids a mismatch.

Accountability, as the flip side of trust, is built into these agreements. It is difficult to trust anyone who is unwilling to be accountable; however, it is also humiliating to be accountable to someone who does not trust us.

Accountability is scriptural. No one could fault Paul for honesty and integrity. Yet he rejoiced that the churches had appointed "a brother" to travel with him when he carried a substantial gift for the Jerusalem Christians who were experiencing hardship.

Paul recognized the need for accountability, especially in the eyes of people who might suspect a misuse of funds.

He writes,"We want to avoid any criticism of the way we administer this liberal gift. For we are taking pains to do what is right, not only in the eyes of the Lord but also in the eyes of men" (2 Cor 8:20-21).

Not only are non-Christians ready to pounce upon any misstep a Christian might make, governments are scrutinizing funding procedures more carefully than they have previously. While in the past Two-Thirds World partners have not been required to make the same in-depth reports that the IRS and agencies in other Western countries demand, more and more non-Western governments are demanding strict reporting of outside funds received.

So important is accountability that the World Evangelical Fellowship is studying the formation of an Evangelical Council for Financial Accountability (ECFA) organization on an international scale.

Accountability of time and money not only helps partners maintain trust but gives opportunity for rejoicing in God's work and provision. Monitoring freely opens doors and books to partner representatives. These visits also enable visitors to see new potential for growth and can unearth problems which ministry leaders themselves may not see because of their closeness to the situation. Mark Hanon, who wrote *Growth Partnering,* an American Management Association publication, says that partners must know the roles they are expected to play and set up control systems to monitor achievement. "Attaining each milestone on plan," he writes, "announces the partnership is working."

Western partners need to be transparent in their reporting of fund-raising and expenses to their partners as well as to their constituency and donors. Lack of trust and poor accountability on either side will destroy a partnership.

7. *Partners must have clear financial policies.*

The greatest obstacle to partnership is that the church in the West has too much of the money. Though money is only one of many shared elements in a partnership, it wields a disproportionate power, primarily because it is overvalued. The New Testament church grew and multiplied, taught and suffered with little reference to trained leadership, budgets and buildings. Money clouds the issue of equality, since it too frequently becomes the dominant factor in a partnership.

A mission leader in the West complained, "Since we control almost all the money, they [Two-Thirds World churches and agencies] almost push us into positions of power because we have it."

On the other hand, a national leader expressed the quandary of Two-Thirds World organizations. "If a man has his hand in another man's pocket, he has to move when the other man moves."

With such potential for misunderstanding, a wise financial policy is an essential ingredient for effective partnership in ministry. There was a period in missions history when giving financial aid was discouraged because it would "spoil" the national church and deprive it of the joy of stewardship. Though this can certainly happen if funds are not carefully and judiciously given, the New Testament clearly teaches responsibility of family members for those in need in the family. Recognizing the financial inequalities between churches, Paul urges the Corinthians to give so that "at the present time your plenty will supply what they need, so that in turn their plenty will supply what you need" (2 Cor 8:14).

How can partners keep money from being a source of power, thereby skewing the partnership out of shape? If a foolproof answer had been reached, there would be a lot more successful partnerships in missions and development.

After years of working through this issue and countless hours of discussion and analysis, several clear guidelines for keeping money in proper perspective have emerged.

☐ Partners must recognize that the ultimate source of all supply is God himself . . . that he is the giver. In his own purposes and wisdom God has chosen to bless some individuals, organizations and societies with a relative abundance of funds, and he holds them responsible as channels for his work. Ownership does not rest with the steward. As funds are released for his work, they return to his control. The ministry receiving funds receives them from God as his provision for their needs, in answer to their prayers, to be used according to his will. This does not limit the responsibilities of being good stewards nor the necessity for accountability. Both are built-in safeguards in this fallen world.

☐ Each partner fulfills his obligations to the other, realizing that money is just one resource. When the value of other contributions is understood and recognized, money can be relegated to its proper importance rather than carrying the heaviest clout.

☐ Partners will not interfere with each other as to how the money is used. This is more easily said than done. How does an organization assure a donor that money designated for a specific purpose will be used in that way without some controls? How are IRS regulations (which require that an organization must be free to use gifts in any way consistent with its purposes in order to issue tax-deductible receipts) to be met without controlling the partners' expenditure of that money? To comply with these regulations, agency boards must make certain decisions about how funds are used.

Third-World churches and ministries are concerned about where the control of money stops. Churches want the freedom to make their own decisions about how funds are used. A suggestion heard more and more frequently is that funds be pooled internationally, and a regional body formed to determine how they are dispensed. But Christians in the West have historically shunned impersonalized giving. And, in fact, with the increasing awareness and involvement of local church mission committees in the West, greater follow-up of gifts is being required, even to wanting to see pictures of the exact results of their donation.

Western agencies and churches need to continue working toward open communications about funding policies. They need to practice trust and noninterference in internal budgets and financial policies of their Third-World partners.

Conversely, Third-World leaders will have to recognize that costs of administration, fund-raising policies and donor communications are essential parts of the financial obligations of the Western agency which generally fall into the sphere of the agency's decision making. Both partners must follow agreed-upon guidelines as to use and reporting of funds.

☐ When both partners have a share in the raising of funds, they each have a sense of mutual responsibility. In Partners International we do all we can to make the needs of partner ministries known to individuals, churches and foundations. However, one of the most vital efforts to gain support and prayer comes through the partner ministry leaders themselves.

At great personal sacrifice and cost to their ministry, leaders agree to spend six to eight weeks every few years in North America, England or Australia representing their own ministries as well as our organization. They see for themselves what kind of information churches ask for and the questions they want answered. They also spend time at our headquarters, and many have remarked about how hard everyone works on their behalf. They understand for the first time what is involved in keeping up mailing lists, sending out receipts, answering phone queries and preparing publications.

They appreciate having partners who are putting out great effort to reach our mutual goal: the building of the church around the world. They appreciate us as their partners, but they also feel that they have helped to raise funds and gain prayer support and thus have diffused some of the one-sided power that they had felt we had.

8. *True partnership demands the sharing of complementary gifts.*

The motivation for partnership goes beyond charity, stewardship or even a commitment to fulfilling the Great Commission. True partnership grows out of the realization that accomplishing the latter cannot be done alone; that we lack certain gifts, skills or resources to complete the task. But we recognize that by combining our strengths with those of others, we can do the job God wants us to do.

When Derk Van Konynenburg decided he needed a partner in his farming business, it was not because he wanted to share the profits or help John make a better living. Derk needed John's skills and expertise, and he wanted the freedom that sharing the workload and responsibilities would give him.

One partner contributes strengths to the partnership that the other does not have, in order for them each to reach the common goal. Paul, our biblical illustration of a model partner in ministry, stressed the importance of differing gifts. He reminded the Roman Christians, "In Christ we who are many form one body, and each member belongs to all the others. We have different gifts, according to the grace given us" (Rom 12:5-6).

The eye and the brain work together to perceive the world around us. While we can live without an eye, what a difference it makes to our understanding of that world. In the same way our national partners could function without our resources or skills, but what a difference our contributions can make in their expansion or effectiveness.

However, as long as Western partners see themselves as only channels for funds or other resources, the partnership remains immature. It is only as we become interdependent upon each other, each offering what the other needs, each receiving what the other gives, that the partnership is truly mature.

A young South African who works on the streets of Johannesburg with tough drop-outs from society told an American audience: "There's no way that you could walk those streets and rap with those kids like I and my team can. There's no way you could build a trust relationship so that they would listen to your message of

Christ. You need us to do what you know needs to be done."

While that is true, the ministry needed funds to launch the program in the community and a partner who would place confidence in the program during its early stages of trial and error. Both members of the partnership took risks and invested their unique strengths in order to see their goal accomplished.

It may sound strange, but Western agencies *need* overseas ministries in order to justify and maintain their existence. And the non-Western agency or church *needs* the help of the Western agency to expand or reach out to new areas. Just as Adam *needed* a helpmate to fulfill his manhood (and conversely Eve needed Adam to fulfill her womanhood) so the Western and non-Western churches need each other to fulfill the Great Commission.

We fulfill each other best in marriage as we complement each other's gifts, compensating for each other's weakness and capitalizing on each other's strengths. So partners in ministry are most effective when they bring complementary gifts to the relationship. Then together we comprise an effective whole.

These resources and skills need not necessarily be equal in quantity or quality, but they must be recognized by both partners as equal in value.

Each partnership will require different resources and strengths, and that's why it's so important to carefully evaluate the relationship before entering into a partnership. For example, Gospel for Asia, which supports nationals in India, does not send Western missionaries overseas. A Third-World ministry that needs the skills of Western workers from its partner would do better forming a partnership with an organization that specializes as a sending agency.

What are the unique strengths that the Western and non-Western churches have to offer each other in complementary partnerships? What do we have to offer that can help us to fulfill each other in ministry?

The Western church's strengths which can complement the non-Western church's efforts are as follows:

☐ A history of the church which dates back to the first century. Though it is marred by war, intrigue, misuse of power and disobedience, it also records heroes, martyrs and great church leaders, a heritage of experience upon which all can draw.

☐ The history and development of missions, rich in victories as well as defeats.

☐ The mission vision of the nineteenth and early twentieth century which has influenced Third-World missions.

☐ Training opportunities and institutions which have provided highly trained leaders for the church and missions.

☐ Administrative skills and structures which non-Western ministries find more and more the need of to function effectively.

☐ Technology (such as radio, computers) which can expand the outreach of a ministry. Many Two-Thirds World countries are rapidly expanding their use of these technologies. Ministry leaders need technicians and training for their staff.

☐ Sources of funding, though shrinking in the West, still represent about 80 per cent of all "Christian money." Western agencies have the advantage of contacts and networking with sources of funding. Other Two-Thirds World countries, such as Korea, are growing in financial strength, but have been restricted in sending funds out of the country.

☐ The vast majority of Christian books have been written and produced in the West. Until more Christian writers and publishers are developed in the Two-Thirds World, most Christian literature in the world will continue to come from the West or be translated from English.

☐ Personnel needs are outpaced by the Two-Thirds World, but thousands of quality young people are available. They can receive some of the best missiological training in the world.

The strengths of the church in the Two-Thirds World which can complement the missions program of the Western church are:

☐ A more holistic world view of God and the spirit world with a realistic awareness of the power of evil spirits. Faith in a supernatural being is the underpinning of most Two-Thirds World societies. This is the thesis of Don Richardson's book *Eternity in Their Hearts,* which seeks to demonstrate that the concept of an all-powerful God has existed for centuries in the hearts of people all around the world.

☐ A lively sense of miracles, of expectancy that God can and will intervene in nature when he chooses. One need only to read the stories coming out of China which describe the thirty years when the church was cut off from all outside contact to recognize this truth.

☐ Interdependent rather than individualistic, the church in the Third World has a deep sense of community and familial responsibility. Over and over the Philippian jailer's story is repeated as a man "and his house" move into the kingdom together.

☐ The national Christian leaders know their culture, world view, language and customs, and can help us understand them. Today missionaries are encouraged to "bond" with a national when they first arrive on the field, taking their cues from the people rather than from other Westerners. Nationals have insight that can avoid mistakes and poor judgments we might make without them.

☐ National Christian leaders bring fresh insights and applications from the Word of God. They share experiences of faith and courage that we in the West may not have known in our own lives.

☐ Most national Christian workers know how to live simple lifestyles. Then, not only can funds be stretched to finance a larger program, but their example is a challenge to those of us in the West who have developed an over-extended lifestyle.

☐ By the year 2000, the church in the Two-Thirds World will provide 162,000 missionaries, if present rates of growth continue (current growth being five times faster than Western missionary growth). Galen Hiestand, North American director for World Evangelical Fellowship, says, "The church's growth is greatest in Asia; its financial resources are concentrated in the west, and its human resources are increasingly located in Africa." Before the end of this century Two-Thirds World missionary personnel will make the greatest contribution to our mission partnerships.

□ The prayer life of many in the Two-Thirds World church is a challenge to our faith. Prayer patterns such as the early-morning prayer meetings of the Korean church, the all-night prayer meetings of the African church, or the twenty-four-hour prayer vigils of a Brazilian mission, can enrich our partnerships.

Complementary gifts are not necessarily stationary. As the Two-Thirds World church develops its leadership and giftedness, it may not need all the resources Western partners now offer. Yet as long as the task of world evangelization is uncompleted, we will need to adjust our relationships so that we can continue to work as partners.

9. Partnership demands sacrificial commitment.

It hardly seems necessary to list commitment as a basic ingredient of successful partnerships since all the other ingredients seem to require commitment as a foregone conclusion. But partnership is fragile at best, and misunderstandings and miscommunications arise easily, especially across geographical and cultural distances. Each partner must have a deep sense of commitment to the other and a desire and willingness to give the benefit of the doubt when difficulties arise.

The partnership will not only be attacked internally but, unfortunately, outsiders are often free to attack the credibility of one partner to the other.

A national ministry came under such an attack from respected Christian leaders within the country. Accusations of misuse of funds for personal gain were made. As stewards of funds given, often sacrificially, by God's people, we must view such accusations seriously. But the Western partner's commitment to the ministry and the recognition of the broad influence it had on the life of the church in the host country demanded that it thoroughly investigate and personally confront the leader. It took travel and time on the part of our staff to sort out the problem and reconfirm the commitment.

It is sometimes difficult, on the other hand, for national ministries to confront or to express criticisms of their partner, especially one that controls major funding for the ministry. The Two-Thirds World partner needs to develop a sense of commitment to the well-being and future of the partner agency and be willing to take risks to help the partner grow and correct weaknesses. As mentioned earlier, it is essential that a forum for personal confrontation and discussion be built into the partnership.

While there is generally a need for long-term commitment in a partnership, partnerships in ministry (unlike marriage) should include a de-partnering process when the mutual goal has been reached. Or the partnership should make mid-course corrections that will target new goals and perhaps change the contributions each makes to the partnership.

One of the greatest weaknesses of West/non-Western partnerships is the danger of dependency upon Western funds. Through the partnership, help should be given to develop local funds. If the original partnership agreement includes a decrease of Western funding within a certain time period, both partners can work toward that goal.

OPPORTUNITY International's policy stipulates that grants for business loans to its autonomous national boards will cease after five years. During that time OPPORTUNITY trains the boards to raise funds locally and from other sources. This fundraising, plus the interest on loans, creates financially self-sustaining agencies that continue making loans for micro-enterprises without further funding from the United States. Of the seven-million-dollar loan portfolio worldwide, only one-third was provided by OPPORTUNITY International. The partnership then continues on a fellowship basis, offering training seminars, encouragement and a network for the independent agencies to exchange ideas.

If de-partnering is not built into the original partnership understanding, dissolution of the partnership could be painful. For example, a national partner ministry decided that it could have greater freedom and less requirements to fulfill if it partnered directly with a major supporting church in the West. The leader simply informed its North American partner of the accomplished change, leaving the partner the task of explaining this to other donors and rebuilding its credibility for other programs. When a ministry becomes independent because it has generated local support, both partners can rejoice. But without a sense of commitment to the Western partner on the part of the national ministry, there is the temptation to look for "a better deal" because of the many contacts the national leader may now have in the West.

On the other hand, when there are no de-partnering criteria, national partners can also feel insecure. They may wonder if boards are going to change policies which will affect their status. When a representative of the agency comes to visit on a monitoring trip, there may be the fear that he will announce withdrawal of funds or personnel.

Both partners must be committed to each other, willing to take risks and make sacrifices to build up the other. But that commitment should have its parameters clearly spelled out and re-evaluated periodically to ensure that there are no unnecessary shocks or that the partnership continues long after its usefulness has worn out.

10. *Partners pray for each other.*

Johannes spent six weeks on deputation in the United States. Within the first week he had a call from his wife in Africa to say she'd had an accident. She was unhurt, but the car had been totaled. Then a cable arrived from his board that the bank had stopped payment on checks because the account had been overdrawn. He was torn between his homesickness and concern for the state of his ministry, and his need to garner prayer and financial support from friends in the United States.

Week after week he spoke in churches, met with missions committees, held home meetings. Sometimes he felt that he couldn't set up the projector and screen and look at his slide set one more time. And though people expressed interest in his vital ministry and responded warmly to his message, few made any concrete commitments. How could he go home empty-handed, knowing how his family and his staff were depending on him to relieve the pressures?

But, while Johannes traveled from church to church seeing little result, his colleagues in his Western partner agency were praying about his discouragement. They were praying for his specific needs: a replacement for his demolished car and a solution to the overdraft problem at the bank.

The last night before he flew home Johannes stayed with one of the staff families. Over the dinner table they discussed these urgent needs, and once again prayed for God's provision.

The next morning Johannes took all his belongings to the office, for he was to fly home to Africa that afternoon. He anticipated the reunion with his family and staff with mixed emotions. He was homesick to see them, but he had little to bring them.

That morning another partner staff member returned to the office after a weekend meeting where, at the last minute, she'd filled in for another national who'd been unable to be there. She had stayed in the home of a Christian businessman, and, in the discussion after the meeting, she shared some of the needs of the national leaders. The businessman's heart responded, and he wanted to become involved. He promised a generous donation, including $16,000 for Johannes's ministry. The news came just hours before he left for the airport. Johannes could have flown home that afternoon "without a plane."

Over and over such answers to prayer are part of the exciting experience of serving God. Prayer is the single most important contribution we can make to our partners . . . the most important ingredient in our partnership.

An Indian couple, both medical doctors, run a medical ministry in one of the most difficult parts of India, where Hindu leaders are fanatically anti-Christian. Dr. Jacob has been called before the magistrate and accused of "converting a Hindu" by promising him financial gain. A Hindu political organization has built its headquarters near the clinic so it can keep its eyes on what goes on and warn patients not to listen to the doctors' religion. Totally surrounded by heathenism of the most oppressive kind, this couple meets each evening after their long day in the clinic for family prayers with their children. They know they must tap the spiritual resources of prayer to face the daily testings in their ministry, and they depend on the prayers of their partners overseas. In spite of the weight of opposition to them, each evening they pray for the needs and spiritual empowerment of their supporting partners and send messages of encouragement when they learn of family or personal trials.

The value of such prayers cannot be counted and certainly can never be taken lightly. Prayer implements partnership no matter what the distance geographically and culturally. Each partner benefits. It's the one ingredient of partnership in which there need be no imbalance, one that each can contribute to the other. Partners in ministry know something of Paul's emotions when he wrote, "I pray with joy because of your partnership in the gospel."

The examples of partnership in missions described in the chapters ahead will demonstrate how these ingredients of partnership come into play . . . more in some than in others. There's still much to learn and more to implement of what we already know. But without question we've entered a new, exciting and, perhaps, last era of missions where we're working together to build the kingdom.

Chapter 6

The Daughter Becomes a Friend

One of the most painful of life's experiences is to have a child who never grows up. Yet, though parents want their children to become independent adults, the adolescent years bring many tensions. Children always seem to grow up faster than their parents want them to, and it hurts to see children make mistakes they could have avoided "if only they'd listened."

The maturing of the church in the Two-Thirds World has brought these same painful tensions. Even though missionaries have talked for many years about "working themselves out of a job," far too few seriously worked at it. Even when mission leaders decreed that national leadership be appointed, property be transferred and churches be responsible for their own finances, there was resistance both among missionaries and nationals.

Consider this model of a ficticious mission agency. The Bible Believing Faith Mission (BBFM) began granting independence to its daughter church in the mid-fifties. Political changes in Parvel increased a nationalistic spirit which the mission could no longer ignore. So the mission began the process of transferring property and reducing pastors' salaries by a percentage each year. But while the missionaries attended the national church conferences, no Parvelians were invited to the annual missionary conference. Missionaries feared they could not discuss matters freely, and it would "spoil the family fun."

At one church conference where discussions seemed to progress in a friendly and cooperative spirit, a more liberal Parvelian told his missionary friend, "You think everything is going well here. But you should hear how we talk about you missionaries back in our own quarters at night." The missionary sadly shook his head, recalling the criticism and even anger he'd heard in the missionaries' barracks.

While the Parvelian church struggled to pay its pastors ("Nobody ever taught us to give," they complained), the missionaries each used the "work funds" *they* had raised for *their* own projects without considering whether or not the church wanted another translation of *Family Life in the U.S.A.* or a new building at the mission campsite (which was too far away for most of the church members to use anyway).

The mission institutions continued to be run by foreigners. While nationals chafed at not being allowed to take over the leadership, for which they were neither trained nor experienced, the missionaries felt no national would ever be really capable of running these institutions and gave little training or "hands on" opportunities to be involved in leadership.

The Parvelian church had independence, all right, but certainly not partnership. It had no access to mission funds, no say over mission projects, no control over the appointment of missionaries in their area. And the missionaries in Parvel lacked the fellowship, intimacy and guidance of wise national leaders who could have enriched their ministry.

Fortunately this model of independence is rare today, but the struggle from paternalism to partnership on the fields has often taken torturous routes.

During the fifties and sixties, missiologists heavily debated which of the following options mission agencies could take:

☐ should the mission turn the work over, move out and consider its work finished?

☐ should it pull out its people and simply send funds?

☐ should it operate under the church?

☐ should it operate alongside the church, maintaining its own independence?

George Peters dealt with this problem at the Green Lake conference, sponsored by the Evangelical Foreign Missions Association (EFMA) and Interdenominational Foreign Missions Association (IFMA) in 1971, warning that no one pattern would work under all circumstances. He counselled:

> But that organization is most ideal which genders the deepest level of fellowship among the brethren, facilitates the freest flow of spiritual dynamics, enhances the speediest and most effective course of evangelism, advances the church in her attainment of maturity, selfhood and identification in the purpose and program of God, expresses most fully the unity and equality of all believers under the same Lord in the same church and in the same family of God."[1]

The SIM/ECWA Model

Since the mid-fifties, SIM (once known as the Sudan Interior Mission) and the Evangelical Church of West Africa (ECWA), the daughter church spawned in Nigeria, have been autonomous bodies. Today its 2500 churches are led by a strong board of African leaders with Reverend Panya Baba as the chairman. ECWA has its own mission board, the Evangelical Mission Society, with over 800 African missionaries working crossculturally, most of them being fully supported by ECWA.

Serving on the church board is one SIM missionary who acts as liaison officer between the church and the 115 SIM ex-patriot missionaries in the country. SIM missionaries are invited by ECWA to serve in Nigeria. ECWA handles visa requests for the SIM missionaries who are asked to teach at their missionary training school, to fill specialized roles in other institutions and to start new ministries approved by the church in unreached areas. Now ECWA wants to more intensely target the cities and has asked SIM to assign missionaries to urban evangelism projects. In this ministry Nigerians and Western missionaries will team up to form an evangelism partnership.

The church, however, does not want the responsibility for handling personnel matters. In essence the church has said, "We don't understand your cultural background. You know all about the relationships with the churches in your countries, so would you please continue to do that."

Taking over the large institutions the mission had spawned was a great challenge for the church. One of the major programs that continued was the network of bookshops, some thirty-six in all. Harold Fuller, Deputy General Director of SIM, explained how this turnover was effected.

"We didn't have pastors run the bookshops because pastors shouldn't be running bookshops or hospitals. We set up a board under the trusteeship of the church with key Nigerian laymen on it. One of them was the Nigerian Trade Commissioner to the U.N. This is the caliber of person they had," Fuller explains.

When it came to the printing press, ECWA asked for a missionary who had been the general manager "because he knows the work and can help developing others."

Fuller explained that whereas the manager had been in charge of the publishing, he now took orders from the Nigerian board. "But he was a man with a very good perspective on national capabilities.

He had worked well alongside the church so he had no problems working under a national board. He had the right mindset," Fuller stated.

Transitional Problems

Though the SIM/ECWA model has developed to the place where the church eagerly welcomes missionaries and the mission feels it is fulfilling a needed role in the country, the transition was not always smooth. "It was about a ten-year process," Fuller recalls. Though some transitions are bumpier than others, certain problems seem to be common to all in one degree or another.

Western missionaries inherited a paternalistic role in which they expected everything to continue to run in the way they had started it. What would happen to the beautiful buildings and the expensive equipment if nationals took over? What would donors think if they saw their sacrificial gifts misused?

Who would handle the books? Because of the holistic world view in many cultures, money is not compartmentalized as it is in the West. What would happen to accountability?

Many missionaries struggled through the process of transition. An attitude of equal partnership was farthest from their minds at that stage.

In fact it was hard to give up a sense of ownership of the ministries which grew out of their vision, whose funds came through their hard work and prayers and which were run with Western efficiency.

At the same time, nationalistic feelings and pride stirred national leaders to demand leadership. It was finally in the open: the mistrust, bitterness and resentment over years of domination.

On the other hand, many nationals feared letting go of the umbilical cord. As one African leader explained, "We always felt that the White missionaries were our masters."

And the older, less educated leadership in the church feared not only the insecurity of letting go of the mission but the changes and threats to their position which would come as younger, more educated national leadership took charge.

CLAME Model in Latin America

Mike Berg, former director of the Latin American Mission, recalls a missionary from another agency asking for suggestions as to how to form a partnership with the national ministries they'd started. "We've been watching you folks," he said, "and we'd like to do what you're doing in a couple of years."

The Latin American missionary laughed and said, "We've been working at this forty years, you know."

The Latin American Mission went through the tensions of transition much earlier than most independent faith missions. Founder Ken Strachan pushed Latin evangelists to the fore in the twenties. By 1945 the church was a completely autonomous body.

But the mission had also spawned a network of far-reaching institutions: a seminary, radio station, schools, a publishing house. By 1970 LAM decided, in consultation with these ministries, to give each its autonomy under a partnership umbrella, the Community of Latin American Evangelical Ministries (CLAME).

Under the CLAME process, ministries were released to national leadership and LAM served primarily as an employment agency, recruiting and sending missionaries as requested by the various institutions. In the early years of the partnership the CLAME office was busy handling property transfers and fulfilling certain services for the partners, such as accounting and public relations. There were high hopes that the institutions would receive large sums of money, but they soon found that LAM was no "pot at the end of the rainbow" which could disburse funds to the other partners.

As the partners grew stronger and their leadership became more experienced, they became less dependent upon LAM and each other. Though still depending upon LAM for personnel and finances, they also developed other sources for their needs.

On the one hand, LAM grappled with its own purpose and redefinition of its role. There was less demand for LAM missionaries as the agencies became more self-sufficient. Would there soon be no need for LAM?

On the other hand, there was disappointment that the agencies continued to be totally immersed in the development and operation of their own institutions and did not become a missionary outreach. As a result LAM began redefining its role and developed its own "Christ for the City" program in which LAM missionaries, by invitation of local churches, concentrated on evangelism and church planting in major cities of Latin America.

In 1985 CLAME dissolved, not in failure and disagreement, but because the partnership was no longer needed. Each of the agencies which survived were strong and functioning. And as so often happens with brothers and sisters in a family, they didn't really have time or interest to keep up with the rest of the family. They had developed their own sources of personnel and funding, much of it within their own countries.

Principles Learned

SIM, Latin American Mission and the dozens of other faith missions that have moved from paternalism to partnership have discovered the following five basic principles that would have made the move easier.

1. *Prepare people with partnership in mind.*

Missionaries going to the mission field today need to be intellectually and emotionally prepared . . . not only to share leadership, but to take a servant role. Their greatest joy should be to see the national church develop leadership and initiative.

At the same time, Western partners will constantly be looking for ways to fill the gaps, meet needs, inspire vision and stretch beyond the abilities of the local church. National church leaders need to

learn to look upon Western missionaries as partners, not patrons
. . . coworkers not competitors.

2. *Be open with everything.*

Keeping finances and decision-making processes secret simply
insures misunderstanding. Partners must be open with each other
if they are going to trust each other.

Harold Fuller recalls an experience while working in Lagos with
a Nigerian who had his Ph.D. When Fuller finally was willing to
reveal his income, the Nigerian with the Ph.D. was surprised to
realize that he was not a well-paid expatriate after all.

CLAME members would never have looked for the "pot of gold"
if they had understood LAM's financial policies from the beginning. If we are afraid to reveal our finances, is it perhaps because
our policies need changing?

3. *Begin to develop a board of nationals right from the beginning
if possible.*

Serving on a board is a great learning experience for everyone.
People learn how others think and how they make decisions by
working through problems together. This is one of the most supportive non-directive means of stimulating leadership maturity.

How board members are selected is also important. The national
church, not the mission, knows who will best represent it. Mission-
appointed board members are often looked upon simply as lackeys.

4. *Define the role of the original mission clearly.*

While SIM retained its right to survey new areas and work with
the church in developing new outreach, LAM allowed itself to be
put in a simple servant role of supplying personnel and money.
Since the most successful partnerships are between two or more
independent organizations who share the same goal, LAM found
its role frustrating and unsatisfying after a time. Its goal to see the
church expand into unreached areas of Latin America was being
thwarted by the internal goals of the CLAME institutions. Fortunately LAM was able to make a mid-course correction which, had

the partnership continued, would most likely have been a complementary role in the partnership.

5. *Be willing to take risks.*

One of the greatest risks in the world is parenthood. After investing twenty years of work, tears, emotional energy and prayer in a child, there is no guarantee that we will rejoice in the outcome. But C. S. Lewis describes the alternative to love in his book *The Four Loves.*

> If you want to make sure of not getting hurt . . . carefully wrap it with hobbies and little luxuries; avoid all entanglements; lock it up safe in a casket or coffin of your selfishness. But in that casket—safe, dark, motionless, airless—it will change. It will not be broken; it will become unbreakable, impenetrable, irredeemable. The only place outside heaven where your heart cannot be perfectly safe from all the dangers of love is hell.

Missions and national churches have also found that exchanging a parenting relationship for a partnering role involves risks. What will happen when unilateral leadership is replaced by joint consultations? What if the results of discussions go contrary to our plans and priorities? What if financial accountability takes second place to culturally accepted monetary practices? What if autonomy opens the door to new ideas, unacceptable influences, even doctrinal shifts?

The Latin American Mission took these risks, and in the process lost one of its partner agencies, the Latin American Seminary, as liberation theology pervaded its staff.

The national church may risk losing its cultural identity, its accepted decision-making practices and even some financial freedom when it partners with the agency that spawned it. But the determination to maintain unilateral leadership, decision-making power, and financial control by the mission or the church may be the greatest risk of all.

Chapter 7

Mainline Models

Mainline denominations have grappled with the question of partnership even longer than the independent mission agencies. In 1947, the International Missionary Council which met at Whitby, Ontario, proclaimed the rallying cry "partnership in obedience." To their credit, mainline denominations took their responsibility of fellowship and fraternal involvement with the "younger" churches seriously.

Many mainline churches, though, have suffered declining membership in recent years, and their mission agencies continue to lose numbers. For example, twenty-five years ago one branch of the Presbyterian Church, the PCUS, had over a thousand missionaries. Today, in spite of the amalgamation of three American branches of the Presbyterian Church, its total missionary force numbers only a few hundred.

While part of this decline was due to theological shifts, a major force was the philosophical change which took place after World

War 2. In desiring to give the national church greater autonomy
and self-direction, missionaries became part of the overseas church
to fulfill the goals of the national church rather than the goals of
the mission board. Most denominational missionaries were no
longer actively involved in evangelism and church planting, but
were able to serve only if invited by national churches, who generally requested their help to strengthen their own programs.

A former Presbyterian missionary explains the philosophy. "We
have a church in every country, so we do whatever they want us
to do. We send missionaries if they invite us. We don't force missionaries on them who are going to do something they don't want
to do."

Where the overseas church was vital and alive, this resulted in an
even stronger church and an effective partnership. Presbyterian
missionaries in Korea worked under mature and visionary Korean
leadership who valued their contributions. The church grew rapidly.

In his book *The Last Age of Missions,* Dr. Larry Keyes quotes
part of Presbyterian missionary Samuel Moffett's 1971 prayer letter
from Korea:

> The Korea [sic] Presbyterian Church already has nineteen mis-
> sionaries spread from Ethiopia to Brazil and more are waiting
> to go. . . . The seminary has just sent one of its best professors,
> Dr. Park Chang-Hwan, the foremost Bible translator in Korea,
> as this country's first missionary to Indonesia.[1]

Indeed, under the guidance of the Holy Spirit, Presbyterian missionaries and the Korean church partnered to build up one of the
fastest growing and most rapidly developing mission-minded
churches in the world.

However, where national Presbyterian churches lack such mature and visionary leadership, they seem to "use" the missionaries
for their own ends. In some Muslim countries, the church demonstrates little ability to reach out to Muslims, and most of the mis-

sionaries are invited to work in service organizations or care for missionary personnel.

A small church could limit Presbyterian outreach throughout the country. The Chilean church, with approximately 1000 active Presbyterians, determines whether Presbyterian missionaries can work with other organizations in the country or develop new ministries there.

A Presbyterian missionary refers to this as "nationalized paternalism. As we nationalized the church, the nationals became paternalistic."

Today the primary focus of missions in the Presbyterian church is partnership, a give and take between presbyteries and churches of different countries. "We are discovering that we no longer can use such language as sending and receiving, donors and recipients," says Bruce Gannaway, associate director for Partnership in Mission, Global Mission United. "One day it will be enough to say simply, 'We share in the common resources that Christ has given us for missions.' " Partnerships include such activities as exchange visits for study and service, and evangelism and new church development, with a strong commitment to ecumenical unity and dialog.

A New Methodist Mission

The Methodist Church has faced a similar decline in membership and missionaries. But in 1984 Methodists concerned about the lack of outreach through the church's mission board established a separate mission agency, the United Methodist Society.

H. T. Maclin, director of the United Methodist Society (UMS), served as a missionary with the Methodist Board. When he left Nairobi in 1971, Emmanuel, his African colleague and dearest friend, came to see him off. Maclin commented on what a great day this was because "we've now become completely nationalized, working in harmony and partnership with each other."

Emmanuel responded with words that Maclin will never forget,

"As long as the world stands, we'll need each other." With these
words still ringing in his ears fifteen years later, Maclin helped start
the United Methodist Society, recognizing that the church is enriched by sharing each other's experiences and lives.

Within a few months after the Society's founding, the Ghanaian
Methodist Church appealed for help. The church had doubled in
the previous eight years and desperately needed Theological Education by Extension (TEE) trainers. Within a few years the United
Methodist Society had seventeen missionaries working in partnership with the church in Ghana.

A unique opportunity for sending an international team developed in Brazil. The Brazilian Methodist Church wanted to begin
a ministry in neighboring Paraguay where only 2.5 per cent of the
population is evangelical. A pastor born in Paraguay had been
working in Brazil for fifteen years, but was now ready to return to
his homeland to begin a church-planting ministry. Would the UMS
help with his support?

At the same time an American Spanish-speaking couple, who
had worked in Bolivia for many years before returning to the United States, was excited to learn about the opportunities in Paraguay.
Sent out by the UMS, they are working with the Paraguayan pastor
under the administrative oversight of the Brazilian Methodist
Church.

Recognizing that salary differences could cause problems, the
Society and the Brazilian church worked out an equitable arrange-
ment. UMS sets the salary for its missionaries and helps them raise
the funds, but the Brazilian church determines the allowance to be
received on the field for both the Brazilian and American missionaries. The difference is held in an account in the U.S.A. for the
couple's use when they return.

Southern Baptists Grow
Over a ten-year period Southern Baptist missionaries grew from

2667 to 3432, a 2.84 per cent yearly increase.[2] Part of the reason might be that all Southern Baptist churches have a commitment to world missions. Another strong influence could be that the mission board continues to see its primary role as evangelism and church planting.

While missionaries are expected to cooperate and be part of the local church and consultation on every decision is vital, "the mission and the conventions as separate entities cooperate without either exercising control over the other," according to Winston Crawley, who wrote *Global Mission,* the official interpretation of Southern Baptist Foreign Missions.

The process of developing independent bodies of Baptist churches or conventions varies from country to country. Dr. Keith Parks, president of the Southern Baptist Foreign Mission Board (SBFMB), explains:

> As the local Baptist organization assumes a stronger responsibility . . . for the denominational or convention development of institutions . . . the mission gradually withdraws itself from leadership roles and moves back into an outreach arm of that convention. . . . Although it can be stated briefly and simply, the complexities are tremendous. . . . It becomes a very complex and sometimes a very painful process.

While the SBFMB is moving into new countries at the rate of more than two a year, where fresh, new relationships and ideal policies can be attempted, in some older fields the lines have been rigidly drawn so that neither the church nor the mission finds it easy to change.

In one southern African country, the convention has gelled into an inward-looking body whose elderly leadership is protective of position and fearful of change, especially by youth. The missionaries are bound to channel any financial or personnel assistance through the convention. When a younger group of spiritually alive and visionary leaders began planting churches, the convention cut them off, and the missionaries could not help.

As Parks warned, retreating from leadership and decision making can be "a painful process."

But in other parts of the world new and exciting crosscultural opportunities face the Southern Baptists. In 1985 the board called for a conference of representatives of conventions who have sent, or have the potential to send, their own missionaries to discuss partnering in crosscultural mission.

The Brazilian Convention, for example, has sent over one hundred missionaries into eighteen countries. It is now consulting with the Southern Baptists about working together in Venezuela.

Portuguese-speaking Brazilian missionaries in Angola could stay in the former Portuguese colony when Southern Baptist missionaries had to leave because of political developments. The Southern Baptists could continue to partner financially with the Brazilian missionaries there, to keep the ministry going until the situation changed and their missionaries could return.

The goal of the SBFMB seems to differ from other denominations. It sees its involvement in the strengthening of the institutions and building up the infrastructure of the denomination as temporary. Keith Parks explains:

As they reach a beginning level of maturity, our feeling is that the training of local leaders and the publication of materials needs to continue, but that really our great burden is to be out on the cutting edge of spreading the Kingdom. As quickly as they begin to emerge where they can do it, then we become partners with them as they focus more on the development of the denomination and the training and literature and institutions, and we become their partner in outreach beyond what they could do without our being there.

Other Creative Denominational Partnerships
Another growing denomination, the sixteen-million-member As-

semblies of God Church, doubles its worldwide membership every six years. Each of the eighty national church bodies is completely autonomous and independent. They are also aggressively reaching out in missions, and this has brought about the need for greater coordination.

Phil Hogan, retired executive director of the Assemblies of God, U.S.A., helped form the International Fellowship of Assemblies of God as a "platform for coordination."

Hogan illustrates the need by pointing to the Assemblies of God Church in Ecuador which has been growing rapidly in recent years.

But now the Assemblies of God of Brazil sends in three missionaries to work in Ecuador. Their next door neighbor, the Assemblies of God of Venezuela, sends one couple across the border. The Japanese, believe it or not, send two couples. . . . The Ecuadorian Assemblies of God says, "Hey, wait a minute. You know, we're glad to have you; the country needs you, but we need some coordinating."

Avoiding duplication of effort was one of the main reasons behind the Presbyterian Church of America's (PCA) Mission to the World. In 1974 John Kyle helped start Mission to the World which forms cooperative agreements with other mission agencies, assigning PCA personnel to agencies that can use their skills.

Mission to the World helps to find the right "fit," offers prayer support and assistance in fund-raising. The partner agency takes over the administrative and ministry responsibilities on the field.

Four years after the mission started, Kyle himself became a cooperative missionary with Wycliffe (with whom he'd served ten years earlier) and later served as vice president of InterVarsity and director of Urbana. Now he's back with his first love, fitting the church's young people into ministry spots overseas where they can function best. John admits, "My parents should have named me John C. Kyle instead of John E.—C standing for cooperation."

John had been an ordained Presbyterian minister in good standing with his denomination, but serving with Wycliffe, he was not recognized as a missionary. Therefore when the PCA split off from the Presbyterian Church U.S.A., the new denomination immediately incorporated cooperative agreements. John says:

> We have the best of two worlds. Mission to the World does not have medical work or aviation services, but we can put a pilot or doctor with an agency that needs them. They serve under the administration of the agency, but fall under the authority of Mission to the World for doctrinal beliefs or moral standards.

Over the years Mission to the World has developed a written working agreement between itself and the partner agency (see appendix). Since PCA is reformed in doctrine, to avoid tension on the field, Mission to the World missionaries are not placed as church planters with a non-reformed mission, but they can serve as service personnel.

How do the supporting PCA churches maintain a sense of ownership when their missionaries serve with many different agencies? This does not seem to be any more of a problem than with interdenominational missions. Kyle says they require regular reports from their missionaries and make every effort to help the churches learn to know and trust the mission agencies represented.

True to his cooperative spirit, Kyle believes that many more denominations should be partnering in this way with other agencies, even to interchanging personnel where needed. Some, such as the United Methodist Society, already form agreements with other agencies, but it's an area of partnering that has barely been tapped.

Chapter 8

Crucified Nationalism

A vant-garde attitudes about global lifestyles color our expectations of the nineties. From business and trade to food fads and international style, the global trends toward interaction and acceptance receive media attention.

ESPRIT, the world's leading sportswear merchant, has proudly captured this international flavor. Doug Tomkins, co-founder of ESPRIT, explains:

> The head of graphics is Japanese; our photographer is Italian; our architects are Italian and French. We have German, Swedish, English, Dutch and Chinese designers. When we all get together, it's like a little United Nations.[1]

From Every Nation and Language

The Bible tells us that in ancient days all people shared the same culture and language. But this uniculture was destroyed at Babel because of the rebellion and self-aggrandizement of the human race. Nations and cultures have distrusted, disliked and fought each other throughout history. Yet, though God punished rebellion with division, one day representatives from all nations and language groups will gather around his throne, singing in harmony in what can only be imagined as a universal heavenly language (Rev 7:9).

It seems fitting, then, that Christians demonstrate a unity and cooperation across cultures. Internationalization of missions is one partnership effort in this direction. Dr. Larry Keyes, president of OC International, tells of two ways that internationalization is taking place: forming partnerships in ministry among diverse societies and forming multinational teams within one society, directed by an international board and funded from global resources. We will look at several models of the latter in this chapter.

Though a number of mission organizations are attempting internationalization, there is still a great deal to be learned about how to develop effective teams and in what situations they function best.

Advantages of Internationalization

Considering how we as human beings resist living, socializing and worshiping crossculturally, it is reasonable to ask, "Why go to all the effort to make something so 'unnatural' work?" Following are two reasons.

1. *Internationalization reflects the supracultural character of the gospel.*

For over two hundred years of missionary activity, Christianity has been seen as a Western religion, bringing with it the customs and mores of Western culture.

But today Christianity is no longer a Western religion. It is truly universal. Thirty-two per cent of the world's population claims to be Christian. There are established bodies of believers on every continent. Black Africa, for example, is over 53 per cent Christian.

Twenty-six African nations have Christian majorities.

With thousands of Christian workers in the Two-Thirds World ready to go as missionaries, it makes sense that Western and non-Western missionaries work together at the grassroots level, as well as at top leadership and strategic planning conferences.

Dr. David Mitchell, Canadian director for Overseas Missionary Fellowship (OMF) believes that international teams are a testimony that the church is one. Dr. Mitchell states:

> We're going to live in heaven as one people. It's great here on earth to see what I think is the real ecumenical movement: those people of many different nationalities and church backgrounds who have a common conviction concerning the fundamentals of the faith.

2. *Internationalization utilizes the complimentary gifts of different peoples and cultures at the grassroots level.*

Putting together an international team must be something like putting together a symphony orchestra. You need different instrumentalists in different quantities for each performance. "Beethoven's Ninth" requires the full orchestra and a mass choir, while Vivaldi's "Four Seasons" requires the exquisite blend of four highly professional string players.

Conceivably an international team could bring together the skills, specialties and inherent personal qualities to meet a specific ministry need.

Imagine, for example, putting together an international team to plant a church in a desperately poor, urban, Black area of South Africa. Perhaps an ideal team would look something like this:

Joe and Karen are a young, Black couple from Birmingham, Alabama. They are outgoing, fun-loving and gifted in personal evangelism. They would be able to identify and empathize with the racially frustrated Black South African youth.

Emil and Carla come from Frankfurt, Germany, where they had their own business. They joined a Christian development agency and spent ten years in Zimbabwe, training small-business people and providing resources for them to develop their businesses. Carla is also a trained social worker and hopes to develop a ministry to women and children through a feeding scheme and classes for women.

Lee and Kim come from Singapore where Lee pastored a fast-growing, mission-minded church. His pastoral and Bible-teaching skills are augmented by Kim's training in Christian Education. His desire is to help the newly planted church become mission-minded right from its inception.

This combination of youth and experience, evangelism, teaching and holistic ministry from three ethnic groups around the world is a beautiful example of supracultural unity and service. But it also carries the potential for major problems.

Potential Problems

Patrick Johnstone, deputy director of WEC International, believes in internationalization. WEC expects to have 20 per cent of its mission force from non-Western countries by the year 2000. WEC's thirty-eight-member Gambian team comes from nine countries.

Johnstone is very candid about the problems:

How can one survive the smell of black beans, dried fish or kimchee, or live with differing cultural values for cleanliness, time, money, leadership expectations and methods of resolutions of conflict?[2]

Following will be four causes of potential problems.

1. *Crosscultural differences.*

A Korean missionary complained about the difficulty of working with American missionaries. The missionary said:

Many Western missionaries carry on their mission work . . . in a one-way direction, from West to East. Their sense of superiority, escapism and stubbornness of their own cultural ways make it difficult to accept joining forces.[3]

Because Westerners have taken the lead for so long, it is difficult for many to serve on an international team without exerting pressure or wanting things to go their way. When British and Americans work together the former want things to go "the way it's done" while Americans want "the most efficient way."

But Westerners are not the only people who are inflexible about their culture or who think it's the "best." Koreans, for example, come from a very unified culture and have little contact with other people, so they sometimes have difficulty adapting in a team situation.

Incompatibility often flares up over seemingly inconsequential matters. For example, a Singaporean and an American were rooming together in Thailand. They had problems when they went out to purchase material for curtains for one of their rooms. The American wanted everything to match; the Singaporean didn't care about matching, just as long as they covered the windows inexpensively.

An Indian team member arrived at the mission office just as several other Westerners were loading up a truck. Glad to see an extra pair of hands, they began to thrust a box in his arms. But the Indian refused saying, "That's women's work." The men were angry with him for his unwillingness to help, and he was disgusted with them for their unseemly actions.

Difficulties arise when families with small children live together. Standards of child-raising vary greatly from culture to culture. What one culture considers harsh and authoritarian, another may describe as biblical discipline.

More serious differences, such as how decisions are made, leadership styles and financial accountability, stretch the unity factor . . . sometimes to the breaking point. It takes a great deal of commitment to the internationalization concept, strong areas of commonality, and Holy Spirit flexibility to make it work.

2. *Financial policies.*

Almost everyone who has had any experience with internationalization agrees that financial policies are the greatest source of difficulty. There are no simple answers to the questions that arise.

Should all the team members receive the same allowance, whether or not they can raise it in their home countries?

Who should set the allowance scales?

Should the team receive allowances equivalent to the local culture?

If Westerners raise their support in their home country and other nationals raise their support locally, how do you avoid the wide discrepancy that is bound to occur?

If all members of the teams are paid on general Western missionary scales, won't they be receiving much more than the local Christians? How do you set salaries of national coworkers from within the country who work alongside the team?

As we look at several models of internationalization later in this chapter, we shall see different approaches to answering these questions.

3. *Time problems.*

Rich Henry of the Central European Fellowship has been involved with a number of international partnerships in developing Christian publishing programs in Eastern European countries. He works closely with Hungarian and Bulgarian leaders. Even before the fall of the communist governments, team members would travel across borders to meet together five times a year. Because of the suspicious nature ingrained into the society through government policies, it was necessary to develop close interpersonal relationships. Henry feels the time required to maintain these relationships is one of the greatest weaknesses of international partnerships.

Fortunately all the members of the literature teams spoke English, but for many Third-World missionaries desiring to become part of an international team, the first requirement is to learn English. After spending several years in language study, the missionaries may still have to learn a local language for ministry.

Combine this with the five to ten years it usually takes to really feel comfortable and at home in another culture (which for the international team members may involve two or three other cultures on the team as well as their ministry culture) and you have a lengthy investment in time just to make the team work. Of course there's no guarantee that relationships will gel happily, and in the end the team may dissolve because members could not successfully bond.

4. *Toxic cultures.*

Secular sociologists are discovering that certain cultures have inbred, historically based antagonisms that continue to surface when people from those cultures work together. Christians have the resource of the Holy Spirit to bring forgiveness and wholeness to relationships.

At a conference at People's Church in Toronto some years ago a Filipino missionary spoke about the ministry in his country. He shared his testimony of how the Lord had met his needs during the terrible years of the Japanese occupation. Sitting behind him on the platform were a group of national Christian leaders, including a Japanese evangelist. As the Filipino turned to go back to his seat, the Japanese leader stood up and went over to him. Throwing his arms around him, he buried his tear-streaked face in his shoulder as he begged, "Please forgive us for the pain we caused you."

God can graciously heal our hurts, but perhaps we should be sure this has taken place before we ask members from "toxic cultures" to work together in a relationship that demands openness and intimacy. Some cultures which fall into this category are the French and English, the Japanese and Korean, and some tribal groups in Guatemala and Africa. A Black South African and an Afrikaaner would need to work through some very recent painful experiences in order to fully accept each other in love. The Lord can and does bring such healing, and when that is demonstrated in ministry it speaks louder than any words could possibly speak.

International Models

Though not a widely practiced concept, more missions are experimenting with internationalization. For SEND International, the concept of internationalization is an overarching philosophy for the whole organization.

On the other hand, other missions are beginning to experiment with internationalization on a smaller scale. The Mennonite Brethren Mission, for example, teamed up a North American and a Brazilian for a church-planting ministry. Each missionary is funded from his own country, and the team is supervised by the Brazilian church.

Hudson Taylor's Legacy

In 1888 Hudson Taylor visited Canada, telling the challenging story of mission work in China. As a result, Canadians, and later Americans, applied to the twenty-three-year-old British mission, and the China Inland Mission became international. Right from the start missionaries from different nationalities worked together, but it wasn't until 1965 that the mission (by then named Overseas Missionary Fellowship) became supracultural, with Asian missionaries serving alongside Caucasians. Today more than thirty nationalities are represented.

With its international headquarters in Singapore, all missionaries go through orientation there. The orientation program is supervised by Japanese missionaries Naoyuki and Izu Makino. "We need to recognize that no one nation is complete or perfect," says Makino. The orientation course develops a spirit of unity among the candidates, though he sometimes finds Americans struggle to accept his advice as an Oriental. Dr. David Mitchell describes this willingness to learn from other cultures as "crucified nationalism."

Once assigned to a team, all members receive the same allowance, which is determined on the field. Funds are received (OMF does not fund-raise, believing that God will supply in response to prayer) in the missionaries' home countries, and they are pooled in Singapore. There each quarter the money is divided according to the percentage that has come in.

When asked if there is resentment if Western missionaries, for example, have all their support come in, but the allowance received is less because the total in the financial pool is short, David Mitchell responded, "There is generally a charitable and generous spirit."

Arnold Lea, now retired after serving as overseas director for eighteen years, was present in 1965 when the doors were opened to accept Asian missionaries. Though it was an exciting development, Lea believes it was difficult for the Asians. They had to adjust to the missionary society and then to the people to whom they were ministering.

Lea still feels it's hard for Asians because OMF thinking remains predominantly Western. Even though each national council is autonomous, coordination and oversight comes through the Singapore office.

Team members, though, find the crosscultural experience stimulating. One American missionary who teaches at a Bible training center in northern Thailand with Canadians, Chinese, Thais and New Zealanders describes the stimulating synergism:

> We have choleric and phlegmatic, practical minded and academic minded, talkers and listeners, preachers and writers. All blend together to provide a balanced diet of teaching and an example for all the students.[4]

Working Toward Servant Leadership

In contrast to OMF, OC International (OC), founded by Dick Hillis, is a relative newcomer to internationalization. But in terms of a determined effort to fine-tune the concept and make it work throughout its nineteen national fields, OC has come a long way.

OC does not develop structures, churches or institutions, but rather helps build the national church through research and training. In a number of cases nationals trained by OC missionaries have been given enough encouragement and help to launch their own ministries. For example, the Philippine Association of Christian Education (PACE) grew out of such assistance, and today is an independent national organization which trains Christian education leaders throughout the country and produces high-quality training materials.

The Philippine Crusades (the name of OC there) has become a strong international team in the last decade, with almost half of the team being Filipinos. Filipino field director Met Castillo also directed the Asia Missions Conference in Seoul, Korea, in 1990, which was jointly sponsored by OC, Philippine Crusades and the Evangelical Fellowship of Asia.

Dr. Castillo received his training at Asbury and Fuller and has built a comfortable cultural bridge to his American colleagues. Many Filipinos tend to be deferential and take a "soft" posture to Americans. But Met has learned to be strong and open, and has earned the respect of his teammates.

Another Filipino team member, Jun Bulayo, has been loaned to DAWN 2000, which is a joint project of the Philippine churches. The goal is to plant 50,000 churches, one in every *barrio* (district), by the year 2000. As of 1990, they were right on track, with some 33,000 churches planted since the early 1980s.

OC President Dr. Larry Keyes would be the first to admit that internationalization has its problems. OC is still studying how best to make it work.

At present its teams on the fields operate under a rather complex, three-tiered system of staff, national missionaries and international missionaries. Nationals appointed as international missionaries fall under the same procedures, regulations and financial requirements as American OC missionaries and, generally, do not work in their own country. International missionaries' financial package is worked out at the OC headquarters, with parity in buying power based on international economic statistics.

Without the usual contacts with churches, friends and family that North American candidates have, nationals find raising funds for their personal support, team and ministry expenses can become a heavy burden. Additionally, how their fellow countrymen view their Western standard of living once they arrive back on the field could be a concern unless they are ministering among upper-class people.

Dr. Keyes also recognizes that international missionaries may find it difficult to raise support in their home countries. Keyes confirms:

> Depending on the manner of recruitment, degree of Western support and amount of dependence upon the missionary's sending church, the "international level" of OC missionaries may discourage the development of indigenous funding for salary support within the sending churches.

In spite of difficulties Keyes believes it is worth the risk. He says:

> Conflicts are a part of internationalization . . . the fact that we, as a mission, have various cultural groups on a team communicates loudly to the peoples among whom we witness. Internationalization increases our credibility and gives us a greater impact overseas than if we were just a Western, North American team of missionaries.

OC teams are also learning how to develop servant-leadership. This is not easy for Americans, who seem to have an inborn desire to "take charge." This is also difficult for Two-Thirds World leaders whose culture has modelled macho or hierarchical leadership, and who feel they will lose respect if they lead by consensus rather than decree.

An OC staff member drove an Indian international missionary to the airport where he would catch a flight for home. The staff member asked, "Well what did you learn while you were here at the office?"

The Indian replied:

I saw servant leadership in action at the OC headquarters. In our villages the chief is the leader and everybody has to do what he says. But I believe servant leadership is right and I want to be that kind of leader.

Being able to observe others modeling scriptural principles is one of the benefits of internationalization and makes it worth the effort. Even though it is difficult, internationalization can work if team members are committed to the concept, each makes a genuine effort to contribute his or her complementary gifts, and each is convinced of the others' equality and worth.

Chapter 9

Great Expectations

J ohn (a pseudonym) was seldom without pain for as long as he could remember. He would never have had any medical care if it weren't for his father, who had gone to the Arabian Gulf to work as a cook. John and his family came from the lowest of the low in India—outcasts with few opportunities for jobs or education.

Yet John's father dreamed that his son would become an evangelist, even when the doctors said he was too weak to study, to work or to marry. God miraculously touched his body, and for a number of years he was strong enough to complete his studies and to marry the educated, Christian *harijan* (outcast) girl his father had found for him. There was always the burden for his own people which drove John to the ends of his strength.

In 1914 another Indian evangelist had that same burden, and through his witness and love for the people, he had established the Bible Believers Mission with more than eighty churches among the outcasts. For the most part they met in simple mud-and-thatch houses of worship, which also served as schools for the impoverished, undernourished children when their parents could afford to release them from the fields where they worked for heavy taskmasters. Life was hard, with scarcely enough food for the families even when every able-bodied adult and child worked from sunrise to sunset. There were the long weeks when the harvest was over and there was no work. The children came to school gaunt, ragged and hungry.

John's family had been part of the Bible Believers Mission and had sorrowed when hundreds of *harijans* turned their back on the church to "reconvert to Hinduism." Indian law had declared special privileges for *harijans* such as education and job training but not if they were Christians.

By the time John finished Bible training, there were only six struggling Bible Believers Mission churches and hundreds of villages without a gospel witness in the area.

John's burden was to take up the leadership of Bible Believers Mission and to develop a church-planting ministry among the *harijans*. Who would help him? The people in the remaining churches were laborers, earning less than one dollar a day when they could find work. There were no other trained leaders; in fact few of the people were literate.

His father, who had been his only source of support for many years, was growing old and weak and would soon have to retire. John's own physical problems had returned, and he needed coworkers who could travel to distant villages and carry on the work when he was bedridden. In spite of these immense obstacles, John took up the challenge.

Then a leading evangelical in India, whom John had gotten to know at Bible school, told him about an organization in the West that assisted indigenous national ministries. He encouraged John to apply, and after months of negotiations and a visit from a headquarters staff person, a new partnership was formed.

This story is illustrative of many of the ministries Partners International assists. Allen Finley, president emeritus who led the organization for twenty-seven years, testifies:

> God has given us gifted leaders who bring dynamic direction to the commitments we have in partnership with thousands of national evangelists, church planters and cross-cultural missionaries.

Over a forty-seven-year history, Partners International has developed guidelines and policies for partnership which are still being refined.

Each of the more than sixty partner ministries differs in background, structure and goals. These are not a group of homogeneous churches which have been spawned by a mission but a variety of ministries in almost fifty countries, most of which grew out of the burden and call of the Holy Spirit to meet a need. The ministries vary from a Bible school in the opium-producing Golden Triangle of Thailand to a Theological Education by Extension (TEE) program for pastors and lay leaders in Tanzania. Though all operate under national boards, some have a dynamic visionary in charge who leads from the front. Others, such as ACRI in the Philippines, runs its youth centers by a strong board of laypeople.

To bring order out of what could be chaos, Partners International has developed a careful selection process, working agreements with each ministry, and a monitoring and enablement program carried out by national regional coordinators.

Careful Selection

Through the selection process both members of the partnership carefully look each other over. Some national ministries have felt that Partners International's requirements are too demanding or limiting and have decided not to form a partnership.

The selection process takes anywhere from a few months to a

year and answers the following questions:

☐ Do we agree on a basic doctrinal statement? Acceptable candidates must hold to Partners International's tenets of faith.

☐ What is the rationale for the ministry? Many national ministries do not have goals and objectives clearly articulated, but they have a general idea of the direction they want to go. Is this in keeping with our purposes?

Though Partners International assists a broad variety of ministries from education to medical work, its primary focus is on church planting among the unreached, and discipling and training for the church. It gives first preference to new ministries who also share these goals.

Partners International also evaluates whether the ministry is strategic in the country or area and what difference it makes in the growth of the kingdom. For example, would expanding a Bible school in an area that already has a proliferation of Bible schools really help to build the national church?

☐ Is the ministry transferable? Can it multiply itself over and over, or would it have to be continually dependent on outside funds in order to survive?

The Evangelical Theological Seminary of Indonesia (ETSI) expects each of its students to plant a church of at least thirty new baptized believers before graduation. Once the church is established it is turned over to the care of the denomination of the church planter, which then provides for its leadership and cares for its growth. One student was able to plant seven churches before graduation.

ETSI provides the training, the encouragement and supervision for its church-planting students, but since it does not become enmeshed in administration and financial responsibilities, it can continue to multiply its ministry.

Operation Lighthouse is transferable. National ministries, however, that are too dependent upon Western technology and expertise or are too oriented toward Western philosophies of ministry are very difficult to multiply indefinitely.

☐ Is the ministry able to operate without outside funding? It may struggle and not be able to reach out or develop new aspects, but generally it should be viable on its own. Independence is preparation for interdependence so that a ministry does not become totally dependent on outside funds.

The Mizos in northeastern India had been headhunters until the tribe came to Christ in a revival led by British missionaries over one hundred years ago. From the beginning they evidenced an unusual concern for sharing the gospel with others. Out of their poverty, women would save a handful of rice from the family meal each day to be given for missions. The Mizos have sent hundreds of missionaries into other tribes. When they targeted the Muslims in Kashmir two thousand miles away, they needed help, and Partners International formed a partnership with them.

☐ Does the ministry have integrity? How does the rest of the Christian community accept it? What kind of relationship does the leader have with other Christians? What are the financial policies and practices?

Partners International does not develop a relationship with a loner, or a ministry that is not accepted by the evangelical community.

In the past it might have been difficult for national ministries to find answers to these questions about Partners International. As the world grows smaller, though, and the Christian community more interrelated, national partners will be asking more and more of these and other questions before entering into a partnership.

Working Agreements

Once the "courtship" is over and both sides agree that they would like to develop a partnership, a written working agreement is developed. Partners International has a generic agreement (see appendix 1) which is a working base for the national board and the national regional coordinator to work through carefully.

Some prospective partners decide that they do not want to be bound by the mission's expectations such as annual audited financial statements, three annual letters from each sponsored worker, ministry information forms completed, deputation requirements and regulations about requesting funds from other organizations in countries where Partners International has a fund-raising council.

What Partners International Expects

Basically Partners International expects the partner to live up to the working agreement. Most partners make every effort to do so, writing prayer letters and reports faithfully and sending audited financial statements annually.

The requirements from the working agreements are not always easy to fulfill. Ministries which have a large number of sponsored staff must see that letters are written at the appropriate time, translated into English if necessary, and mailed to the Partners International headquarters in California. Sometimes letters are lost. Occasionally nationals fear that prying officials in hostile countries might intercept the letters and, thus, jeopardize the ministry, so they are very cautious about what they report.

One African leader complained about the many requests for information from Partners International:

I wish the Lord could provide money so we could hire someone to sit down and do the paperwork on our behalf. We started out as preachers, full of zeal for the work of the Lord. . . . We may not be able to fulfill all the writings that you expect from us.

But while this is a recurring complaint, Partners International realizes that donors and prayer partners deserve information as they continue to be involved in these ministries. In fact in recent years churches and individual donors have increased their expectations of reports and letters. But staff sometimes go to national partners "hat in hand" asking for one more report, knowing how busy they are.

Confidence Factors

Partners' expectations of its national partners are reviewed regularly through an established monitoring process. This is not simply an evaluation of accomplishments and procedures. Rather, it is an opportunity for the leader, board and the regional coordinator to assess "how are we doing?" and "what will help us do better?"

Four "confidence factors" are part of this regular monitoring process.

☐ The partner ministry must have a governing board that is informed, involved and responsible.

A regional coordinator and several Partners International staff met with an African board in relation to a ministry where accountability and use of designated gifts were in question. As the very capable and experienced board of men and women listened to the discussion, a government official on the board interjected, "I see, you are expecting us to be an operational rather than an advisory board. We'll have to decide whether we can take that responsibility."

In this case, since the board members had great confidence in the leader, they had been more or less rubber stamping his decisions. But as the problems and needs of the work were openly discussed, they recognized that he needed their expertise, advice, and more of their control.

In strongly hierarchical cultures where leadership is vested with a great deal of power, the acceptance of the concept of "governing boards" over leaders often requires an educational process. As long as Partners International sees this process developing, it increases its confidence factor in the ministry.

☐ The partner ministry must have goals and objectives that are clear, measurable and achievable.

This Western business concept has now permeated the world. Two-Thirds World ministries, however, sometimes still have problems setting goals.

For example, a principal of a graduate school overseas told his faculty, "I don't know how you can say that the Holy Spirit is going to bring 200 new students to us in the next five years, but," shaking his head with a wry grin he added, "if you say so, I guess it's all right with me."

Many national leaders and their boards appreciate training and help in setting goals and objectives for their ministries. As the staff of Partners International sees this effort growing, their confidence factor increases.

☐ The partner ministry must have policies and procedures which guarantee that the funds are being spent for the purpose for which they were given. This means that appropriate accounting and financial management procedures must be used.

This pressure comes not only from Partners International but from their governments. In India, for example, ministries must turn in detailed accounts of all overseas funds received. No overseas money may be used for any publication purposes, so if a ministry has a magazine or other publication, it must make sure to keep funds in separate accounts. On a number of occasions our regional coordinator in India, Dr. B. E. Vijayam, has been able to sort out the confusion and intricate government requirements and save a ministry penalties and even forfeiture of funds.

When projects are in process, donors require pictures and updates to know what their funds are accomplishing. Keeping these reports flowing and providing a clear, well-organized financial statement annually increases our confidence factor.

☐ The partner ministry must have the personnel necessary to put into practice its policies and procedures.

With the growing number of trained Christian workers around the world, this should be less and less of a problem. Often our partnership makes the difference between having sufficient qualified staff and operating with a skeleton crew.

Project 2000, a Partners International-sponsored program which enables nationals to plant churches in unreached areas, opened the door for many ministries which had longingly discussed sending an evangelist or team into such an area. They even knew the right people to do the job, people who felt the call for such pioneer work. But there were simply no funds available to add another worker.

With Project 2000, the partner ministries were encouraged to research these unreached communities. What kind of people lived there? What kind of approach would be best to enter the community? Knowing something of the cultural and religious climate of the area, how long would it take to plant a church? What would it cost to keep a worker or workers there for that period of time?

When these Unreached People Profiles are returned to headquarters, Partners International finds churches and individuals in North America eager to underwrite them and can then inform the ministry, "Hire your workers; send them into the new village; God has raised up a special partner for your need."

As the staffs of dedicated and capable workers develop so that the work can carry on effectively, our confidence factor increases.

What Do the National Ministries Expect?

Since the Bible Believers Mission began receiving assistance from Partners International, the board has taken on twenty-five church planters, and in the past eight years more than thirty churches have been established.

When a staff member from the Partners International office visited John, he proudly took them to a little print shop in town. "I was able to purchase the press with a small loan from the government," he explained. Never mind that the press was an old lead-type, hand-operated machine . . . high in manpower and low in quality. The shop provided several jobs for *harijan* families, and the profits paid for a magazine for the churches. Young people are reading now, and John felt it was time that the *harijans* had their first magazine written by and for them.

The Bible Believers Mission hired its staff, started churches, made a loan, purchased equipment, and started a small business and magazine, all without reference to Partners International. These ministry decisions are theirs to make and, if the projects fail, they deal with them themselves.

That's the way the nationals like it.

Allocation of Funds

While national ministries are responsible for internal funding, they send additional budget requests and project needs for approval to the coordinating office of Partners International. They would *like* to see those budgets and projects fully funded. But they are also aware that Partners International must raise these funds by approaching churches, individuals and foundations with the needs. There is no funding pool just waiting to be divided up as requested. Thus, on the basis of general income, health of the ministry's account and a sense of God's leading, the international team must decide whether all or a percentage of the budget can be provided in the coming year.

National boards also understand that Partners International itself, has expenses for staff, communications, fund-raising, financial management, field travel and whatever it takes to service their needs. While these funds are generally raised by missionaries as part of their support package in traditional agencies, Partners International covers its expenses primarily from a percentage taken from each ministry's funds.

An in-depth survey of over 500 Christian non-profit organizations in the United States revealed that support service expenses average 20-25 per cent of income. Partners International are 3 to 8 per cent below the average mission agency.[1]

Communication the Key

National leaders don't expect to become involved in internal affairs at Partners International except when major decisions which affect their ministries are made. This fact came to light very clearly when the newly appointed Regional Coordinators were introduced at the International Conference of Partners International in 1987. At this joint gathering of the national leaders, dissatisfaction surfaced about what was seen as a "unilateral decision." "We should have been consulted" was the general cry.

Since then two national leaders have been added to the international board to give greater voice to national ministries in such situations, another step forward in the partnership learning process.

Missions such as Gospel for Asia, World-Wide Mission, Christian Aid and others have also grappled with fine-tuning partnerships with national ministries. More and more organizations are finding this can be one of the most gratifying relationships.

Two-Thirds World cultures tend to be more relational than Western cultures. When asked what they expect of partnership, national leaders respond:

Partnership is not supposed to be one way. It's a two-way partnership . . . exchanging ideas, staff, information and resources.

We shouldn't write off people when they do not do things the way we do them. In that we may be losing each other in the relationship . . . there needs to be sensitivity.

People from headquarters used to come and sit down and talk with us, and make us feel like a brother . . . paperwork is good, but we believe in the personal touch.

Folks up there, the staff and board, should listen to what we say and then ask, "How can we get together on those ideas?"

Meeting the Expectations

Obviously, with such a wide divergence of people and cultures and with the heavy pressures of keeping national ministries and prayer and financial partners satisfied, Partners International staff will be unable to meet every expectation.

But Professor B. E. Vijayam is trying. "Viji," as he is affectionately known, grew up in a Christian home in India and had the benefit of an excellent education. He earned his Ph.D. in geology from Osmania University and later was a Fulbright Scholar at Northwestern University. He served with the Indian Department of Science and Technology and the National Institute of Oceanography while working as head of the department of geology at the university in Hyderabad. He and his Ph.D. candidate students were instrumental in discovering oil, which helped change India from being 70 per cent dependent on foreign oil to only 20 per cent dependent. He also was involved in the discovery of the largest vein of coal in India.

But through these years of success and accomplishments, Dr. Vijayam had a driving desire to serve God. For many years he served on one committee after another, generously giving of his time to such organizations as Youth for Christ, the YMCA and the Hindustan Bible Seminary. But deep in his heart he wanted to fulfill his evangelist-father's dream and go into full-time ministry.

In June 1988, Professor Vijayam took early retirement from the University of Hyderabad to become Regional Coordinator for Partners International. In this capacity he would be able to help, build up, pray with and evaluate the ten partner ministries in India and Bangladesh which are associated with Partners International.

Professor Vijayam had another dream. In his spare time he had worked on a series of agricultural experiments to enable impoverished villagers to develop a livelihood. He'd studied self-help projects and knew, for example, how to point starving cobblers into a more lucrative home-tanning business. (Only certain Hindu castes, like *harijans,* will work with leather in India.)

Having had a lot of experience with government agencies over the years, he not only understood government policies, but knew influential people upon whom he could call for advice.

And through the years he'd become an astute student of the Word of God, able to teach and apply its truths in the Indian culture, simply but profoundly.

Dr. Vijayam cared deeply about the partner ministries with which he worked. On his first visit to the Bible Believers Mission he noted John's pain and extreme exhaustion, even as he took him from one village church to another. He urged John to go to the hospital and consider heart surgery which could now possibly correct the problem he'd suffered from all these years. Over John's resistance, the professor made arrangements for him to travel the several hundred miles to the hospital. Then he contacted the Partners International headquarters, asking for prayer. He alerted them that surgery might be forthcoming and that funds would be needed.

Prayer partners in the U.S.A. rallied around John, providing funds for the surgery (about one-tenth of the cost it would have been in the U.S.A.) and praying for him during the months of his setback and recovery. Dr. Vijayam himself made the 700-mile trip to the hospital to visit John. After John's recovery, Dr. Vijayam and another Christian professor spent a week teaching the Bible Believers Mission workers. These harijan Christians were overwhelmed that high-caste men, men of such wisdom and stature, would bother to come and train them.

The Bible Believers Mission really exists under another name, and it is but one of a network of indigenous ministries led by godly men and women whom God has endowed with vision for his work. Partnership with them fulfills our greatest expectations.

Chapter *10*

Testing the Waters

T he "Valley of Blessing," headquarters of the Antioch Mission, led by Rev. Jonathan dos Santos, a Brazilian pastor and visionary, is located in the verdant hills thirty-five miles from São Paulo, Brazil. Here missionary candidates from Brazil and other Latin American countries are trained to serve crossculturally. Founded in 1975, the mission has sent out more than forty-five missionaries to such faraway places as Israel, Angola, India . . . and Albania!

Facilities at the Valley are simple: cement block dormitories where a dozen students crowd into a room which should house four. Before the new dining hall was built this year only a fraction of the staff and students could be seated at one time, which made mealtimes on rainy days a challenge. Everyone lives "by faith," trusting God to supply their needs week by week.

But this is just the kind of missionary training Santos values. He knows the Brazilian church will not be able to provide high allowances, nor will the government allow transfers of large sums of money out of the country. "Brazilian missionaries already know how to live the simple lifestyle," Santos explains.

Coming from a position of powerlessness, as Jesus chose to do, might be just one of the unique advantages missionaries from the Two-Thirds World have as they fan out across the world. Western values of advanced educational opportunities and financial and political power have often built a wall between the church and the missionary.

In spite of limitations of such resources non-Western missionaries have grown from 13,000 in 1980 to 36,000 in 1988. Larry Pate, author of *From Every People,* projects that at current rates of growth, an estimated 86,500 missionaries from Two-Thirds World countries will be serving crossculturally by 1995, and there will be almost 2000 non-Western mission agencies by the year 2000. At present there are some 85,000 Western missionaries serving in foreign countries, but 42 per cent of them are short-termers. Non-Western career missionaries are growing at five times the rate of Western missionaries and will surpass them in numbers before the turn of the century.[1]

Will History Repeat Itself?

The leaders of these Two-Thirds World agencies have not sprung up overnight. Many have attended the international congresses and consultations, have studied in the West and have worked with Western missionaries. They've heard the partnership rhetoric and, indeed, are promoting it.

In an article for *Missionasia* Filipino leader Dr. Met Castillo writes:

The natural and logical outcome of interlinking the various Asian mission agencies and boards are concrete forms of mission partnerships. The vast number of unreached peoples in Asia, and the complexity of the mission task, compounded by the chain of missional problems call for the pooling of mission resources and personnel.

But though there are many commendable instances of partnership in the West, Two-Thirds World leaders can still point to the proliferation of Western mission agencies, more than 700 at latest count, and duplication of efforts. Rather than cooperating with existing bodies, Westerners continue to develop new independent missions organizations.

It will come as no surprise to learn that cooperation and partnership are just as difficult to implement among Two-Thirds World agencies as they are in the West.

Will They Partner with the West?

In his 1980 survey of Two-Thirds World agencies, Dr. Larry Keyes asked to what degree these missions desired to cooperate with other Two-Thirds World agencies and with the West. Mission leaders from all regions answered they would like to cooperate with others, but particularly with other non-Western agencies.[2]

Experience has taught these Two-Thirds World mission leaders that Western missionaries tend to take control and that non-Westerners may too easily accept structures and teaching that are foreign in their society because of their poor self-image and/or lack of training.

Reacting to these dangers, Dr. David Cho, president of the Asia Missions Association and the newly formed Third World Missions Association, declared:

> We must boldly remove the obstacles hindering Christian mission. We must remove all remnants of Western culture, Western colonialism, Western methodology and Western thought from Asian theology, doctrine, churches, structures and methods.[3]

Though Dr. Cho has expressed disappointment in the lack of cooperation on the part of Western missions, he values the gifts and abilities of Western Christian leaders. He asked Dr. Ralph Winter to share the platform with him at the very conference where Cho spoke on "De-Westernizing the Asian Christian Movement." His concern is to solidify and strengthen the Asian, African and Latin American mission base, not "to form an anti-Western force."

His fear is rather that the Two-Thirds World missions will lose their self-identity and become even less acceptable to the masses of people who have resisted the message of missions for so long. He stresses that Paul made it clear in his epistles that the church must be rooted in the culture and ethos of the people.

Wade Coggins, executive director of the Evangelical Foreign Missions Association (EFMA) for many years, recalls watching the tenuous steps of growth and partnership between Two-Thirds World missions and their Western counterparts. While meeting with representatives of fledgling Brazilian missions in the mid-seventies, he realized:

> We weren't talking about the control of the mission over the church or the church's control of the mission. We were talking as people both committed to the concept of world evangelization. And that the old missions and the new missions ought to talk about what they could do together.

This was in contrast to most discussions between church and mission leaders in those days. Coggins said: "I realized that the way out of the church mission dilemma that had been with us so long was an outward look."

But having lived through the church/missions tensions of the sixties and seventies, Coggins also understands the reticence of Two-Thirds World agencies to trust us for fear we'll take over and impose our methods and values. "Talking about partnership is easy," Coggins says. "We've come through the euphoria. . . . 'Man this is marvelous.' The tough questions are ahead of us. Most of it's going to be two organizations sorting it out for themselves."

And the task of educating the churches and missions candidates is far from over. Our ethnocentricity clings to us like a wetsuit, and the deeper the differences between cultures, the "colder" we seem to become.

One wonders at the audacity of an American college student going overseas for a short term "to train native pastors." It is this self-confidence and assurance that we have all the answers that frightens people like Dr. Cho.

Western and Non-Western Agencies Partner
In the mid-nineteenth century the Karen Christians in Myanmar (formerly Burma) formed one of the early non-Western mission agencies, the Bassein Home Mission Society. With help from the American Baptist missionaries, they sent Karen missionaries to work among the Kachins, a tribe living several hundred miles away.

More than one hundred years later, John and Helen Dekker, missionaries with the Regions Beyond Missionary Union in Irian Jaya, encouraged the fledgling church among primitive Danis to take the message of Christ to neighboring and often hostile tribes. Within a few years sixty-five Dani couples, fully supported by the gifts and prayers of Dani Christians, were in service. Though nobody even thought about formal partnership arrangements, Dekker provided the complementary encouragement, training and counsel the Danis lacked.

With little cash income, the Danis needed to develop a means of funding their growing missionary force. Dekker introduced peanuts, and the income from the crop financed much of the church's missionary outreach. Without peanuts, the missionary effort would have been hopelessly strapped.

Today some Western mission agencies are developing more formal partner relationships with Two-Thirds World agencies. For example, SIM has drawn up an agreement with the Indian Evangelical Mission and others to work together to recruit and support missionaries in Africa and Latin America where SIM serves (see appendix 1).

The Indian missionaries are expected to raise funds and prayer support within India for outgoing airfare, baggage allowance, equipment needs and so on, as well as furlough and medical expenses while in India. SIM arranges deputation for prayer and financial support for the balance of their needs and while on the field the missionaries come under the direction of SIM.

Such co-sponsoring will become more and more urgent as the numbers of Two-Thirds World missionaries grow. Larry Keyes discovered that 35 per cent of these missionaries do not receive their promised salary. Part of the problem is due to poor administration and distribution and part to a need for better stewardship education in the churches.

A very real part of the problem is the lack of a strong financial base, in fact, bankrupt economies, in many of the countries where mission vision is growing fastest. And though Two-Thirds World missionaries may "know how to live simply," according to Jonathan dos Santos, the cost of living may be much higher in the country of service than at home. A Brazilian missionary working among Muslims in Germany could not live on his Brazilian allowance, no matter how simply he or she lived!

When the Iglesia Nazaret and El Escalon, two mission-minded churches in San Salvador, partnered to form the Salvadoran Evangelical Mission, the civil war was at its height. Over 40 per cent of the population was without work, and the economy was in shambles.

But the SEM determined to send its first missionary couple to Spain to begin a church-planting ministry there. People gave sacrificially but could not provide all that their missionaries, the Bustamantes, needed to live in Spain. They approached Partners International to form a co-sponsoring relationship, whereby donors in the United States matched SEM's contributions.

Such financial partnership not only enabled SEM to send the Bustamantes but encouraged Christians to give sacrificially so that within a few years several other missionaries had been sent to an Indian tribe in Guatemala, and the first school for the deaf in El Salvador (a totally unreached segment of the population) was opened.

Other Ways to Partner

In spite of the difficulties and fear of repeating past experiences, Two-Thirds World agencies realize that working together with Western agencies can better help them reach their mutual goal. Following are other forms of partnership which are emerging:

☐ *Training partnerships*

As the Africa Inland Church Mission Board (AICMB) grew, the need for training African missionaries in mission strategy and methods became more urgent. Bible school and seminary training did not prepare their missionaries for the challenges of crosscultural and church-planting ministries. Yet the AICMB did not have trained and experienced teachers to run such a school. So it turned to its parent organization, the Africa Inland Mission, to partner in establishing a missionary training school. The school remains under the leadership and control of the AICMB, but AIM missionary teachers help staff it.

As more and more non-Western missionaries volunteer to serve crossculturally, creative training partnerships will have to develop in order to avoid sending inexperienced and untrained non-Western missionaries to repeat the same mistakes earlier Western missionaries subconsciously made.

But Western trainers will have to be willing to adjust their philosophies and methods to adapt to the cultures where they are teaching. To avoid repeating the North American models of Bible schools and seminaries, which have not necessarily been effective, a lot of hard questions have to be asked and a teachable spirit demonstrated.

Excellent training programs have developed in various parts of the Two-Thirds World, and interchanges of faculty and students offer an exciting potential for the future of missions training.

On a less formal level Jonathan dos Santos, pioneer in training Two-Thirds World missionaries, responded to the urgent need for training in Eastern Europe after the political changes allowed for freedom to travel and communicate. When he learned of the dearth of trained leadership for the Romanian Church, he offered to care for and train six Romanians at the Valley of Blessing if they could get to Brazil.

☐ *Research partnership*

Where will all these new non-Western missionaries serve? How will they avoid the endless duplications of the past, such as establishing a Baptist church, Bible church and a Presbyterian church in one small town?

The mission world has adapted the tools of research to discover where the churches are and where the unreached can be found. And agencies in the Two-Thirds World are quickly taking advantage of the benefits of research as they plan their evangelism and church-planting strategies.

But research is expensive and exacting and requires sophisticated equipment if done on a large scale. Here is an area where Western agencies can make their expertise and equipment available, without the temptation to manipulate or interfere with the use of the data.

In the months preceding COMIBAM (Congress on Missions in Ibero-America), the continent-wide missions congress held in São Paulo, Brazil, in 1987, hundreds of researchers fanned out across Latin America asking questions to analyze the state of the church. Each country had its own COMIBAM committee which was responsible for finding researchers and for getting the data together.

But without the Global Mapping Project located at the Center for World Missions in Pasadena, this data could never have been analyzed and made available. With highly trained personnel and sophisticated equipment, Global Mapping Director Bob Waymire and his associates were able to put all the major data on computerized four-color maps which visibly illustrated the concentrations of unreached people, the major language groups and the evangelical population.

Working under tremendous deadlines, the COMIBAM team in Guatemala was able to deliver the "Atlas de Comibam" in time to be distributed to the more than 3000 delegates at the conference.

This was indeed a partnership on a massive scale which yielded immediate and visible results and enabled each national group of churches to inspire and challenge their own constituencies and plan their mission outreach.

Other national research agencies, such as the Church Growth Research Center in Madras, India, and the Ghana Evangelism Committee in Ghana, partner with denominations and missions to help them plan their outreach programs.

☐ *Partnering through conferences*

In May 1990 the Latin American Consultation on Muslim Evangelism (CLAME 90) met in Miami, Florida. This consultation grew out of the Latin American church's growing interest in Muslim evangelism, as evidenced at COMIBAM. The Holy Spirit seemed to convict Christians in different parts of the continent that Latins could have a special advantage working among Arabs.

Because of 400 years of Moorish domination of Spain, Latin Americans share many of the same physical characteristics, cultural traditions and even language similarities with the Arabs. Politically, Latin Americans hold no threat or historical animosity for the Arab nations.

Since COMIBAM, Latin American missionaries have gone to Pakistan, India, the Middle East and Europe to work with Muslims.

CLAME 90 met to discuss the feasibility of sending 100 Latin American missionaries to the Arab world by the year 2000.

The conference was unique in its representation. Co-sponsored by the COMIBAM office in São Paulo, and Project Magreb, an indigenous Latin American mission in Argentina, a good proportion of the ninety-five delegates came from the Southern Hemisphere.

North America was represented by delegates from the Zwemer Institute and Frontier Missions, both of whom are involved in Muslim ministries, and they already work together closely at the Center for World Mission.

A number of leading Arab Christians from Middle Eastern and European countries added their insights to the conference. At the conclusion, one Arab brother stated:

> This meeting is historical. This is the first time anybody has asked our opinion about coming to our part of the world and we welcome it, and we welcome you, the Latins.

The lack of training to reach Muslims was recognized as one of the main obstacles, and training seminars across the continent were initiated. The North American delegates indicated their willingness to help where needed.

As a closing challenge, the Arab delegates commended the cooperative spirit and urged the Latins to send people who are "willing to make mistakes." But before sending missionaries, they want leaders to come and look over the situation, to know what training and ministries are already functioning, and to base their plans on what they've learned.

"Design a vision group," they recommended. "Send people on tours and we will help them understand our situation and our people." This kind of partnering through conferences should certainly pave the way for more effective long-term partnering in future ministry.

Two-Thirds World Partnerships
On the other hand, the breakdown of long-term relations in missions has paved the way for new partnerships.

When the Indian government began denying visas to missionary medical doctors and other medical personnel, mission hospitals in India began closing down, for they had limited funds to hire national staff. It was at this time that the Emmanuel Hospital Association was formed, bringing together almost twenty Christian hospitals into a partnership for survival. The association offers administrative and financial assistance by serving as a channel for foundations and other agencies to provide funds.

John Richard, former executive director of the Asia Evangelical Association, believes, "It's one of the best patterns of partnership in my limited experience."

More and more Two-Thirds World partnerships are emerging as Christian leaders realize that chances of survival along with effectiveness increase as they close ranks.

Dr. Bong Rin Ro, dean of the Asia Graduate School of Theology, defines another reason for partnership in the area of theological education:

> We are trying to train Asians in Asia, within the Asian context because of the high percentage of brain drain. Among Chinese from Taiwan the brain drain has been 86% in the last twenty years; among Indian theological students it has been about 90%. . . . For various reasons they don't go back. Asia has lost a large number of church leaders. We have 1000 seminaries and Bible schools in Asia, but we don't have enough lecturers.

To confront this need, the Asia Graduate School of Theology (AGST), a consortium of seventeen graduate seminaries in four countries was formed in 1984. Accredited by the Asia Theological Association, these schools offer four degrees, including the Doctor of Ministry. By banding together and allowing for interchangeable credits and exchange of students and lecturers, Asia Graduate School can offer degrees which are internationally recognized and of a high quality.

"Through the cooperation among evangelical seminaries we are able to offer this post-graduate school," Dr. Ro explains. "Otherwise not many people would recognize the post-graduate degrees offered by the individual schools."

In 1989 the Alliance Biblical Seminary in Manila, a member of the AGST, graduated its first doctoral students. The seven graduates came from Indonesia, Taiwan, the Philippines, New Zealand and one from America . . . a missionary.

Dr. Ro recognizes that each Asian country has its own culture, and it would be preferable to study within the students' own cultural context. But he explains, "We can't afford to set up doctoral programs in each country. We don't have the professors or the research materials." However, he admits that the AGST program is more culturally relevant than a Western education because of the common ground shared by the Asian cultures.

Korean Missionaries Partner with Thais

It's this "invisible cultural link" which has drawn missionaries of the Korean International Missions to partner with the Church of Christ in Thailand in evangelism and church planting.

Koreans and Thais share the same Confucian/Buddhist background. They think similarly, believing that everything that happens has a spiritual cause. They share the virtue of conformity and filial respect ingrained for centuries. Thus the pastor carries enormous authority. Both cultures value the courtesy of saving face and seek to avoid offense by confrontation.

The Korean International Mission (KIM) began working in Thailand in 1956. But in recent years missionaries have sought to work in partnership with the Church of Christ in Thailand (CCT), which is an ecumenical body representing a number of denominations and parachurch agencies.

In preparation for working together the joint committee planned a unique exchange program. A Thai evangelist was brought to Korea to study at the East West Center for Mission Research and

Development for one year.

Later a group of Thai Christian leaders attended the World Evangelism Crusade in 1980 and visited many Korean churches and projects. As a result, one of the Thai leaders established a prayer mountain for twenty-four-hour prayer vigils and fasting, based on the Korean model he'd seen.

KIM board members and Korean pastors visited Thailand for a week to see the work firsthand and get to know the people better, while the CCT executive committee visited Korea and also attended church growth seminars there.

Korean missionary Jung Woong Kim observed:

The more pastors, elders and women leaders visit mission field, the better the Korean church's understanding of the Thais and missionary work.[4]

Koreans are learning the meaning of "cha cha" (slowly, slowly) as they find church growth does not respond as rapidly in Thailand as it has in Korea.

Both Korean and Thai workers are recognizing some of the following principles that will have to be applied as Two-Thirds-World mission agencies around the world develop partnerships:

☐ Cultural imperialism is just as likely to tarnish Two-Thirds World missionaries working in other cultures as it has Western missions. It should be remembered that North American missionaries share cultural roots with Europeans, but they are not immune from this accusation even there.

☐ Two-Thirds World missionaries need to be wary of pride of accomplishment. For example, the rapid Korean church growth and well-documented early-morning prayer meetings could cause Korean missionaries to look down upon churches in other cultures who do not experience these.

☐ Two-Thirds World agencies and their supporting churches will have to understand the extent of the responsibility they assume when sending out missionaries, so that they are faithfully and consistently backed by finances and prayer. Some of the high rate of fall-out among Two-Thirds World missionaries is due to the lack of adequate and regular support from their home base.

☐ Constant shift of missionaries and changing strategies weakens the effectiveness of the ministry. Kim writes:

> Missionaries change their areas and adopt different approaches depending on the missionary's interest and concerns. There is often no connection between a missionary's work and his successor's.[5]

As Two-Thirds World boards become more experienced, such problems should become less common. They will no doubt face many of the same obstacles Western agencies have faced. But hopefully they will learn more rapidly than the West has, that the right kinds of partnership will serve as cords of victory to strengthen their impact on the lost around them.

Chapter 11

Increasing the Risk Factor

When you think of missions, what's the first word that comes to your mind? It probably isn't *innovation*.

We've seen from our analysis of various partnerships, that needed change has come slowly. Though a lot of missions recognize the value and importance of partnership, they hesitate to implement it because of the risk factor.

There are a growing number of agencies, churches and individuals, however, who are consciously seeking innovative ways to reach out to the 3.3 billion people who live in the restricted world—restricted politically or because of societies and religions which are hostile to Christianity. They recognize that straying from the traditional forms of mission work may result in failure, in spending precious mission funds without results and in subjecting themselves and those involved in their programs to criticism. But the urgency of the task of world evangelization drives them to ask God to show them other ways to share the gospel, particularly in those regions where the message of Christ has had little or no impact.

This is not to say that traditional mission agencies are not strategizing for the twenty-first century. This is the day of "long-range planning" and there are few organizations of any size who have not taken time to develop five- and ten-year plans. The decade which launches us into the twenty-first century has added an additional impetus to the already strong influence of the businesspeople on boards and committees. Most missions have commendable plans and goals for A.D. 2000.

However, like giant ocean liners changing course in mid-ocean, mission agencies take a long time to turn around. The constituency in the home country, the long-term career missionaries and the established church on the field can act either like ropes pinning Gulliver down, or like climbers' guidelines to see that they stay on the right path to the top.

Yet outside the more traditional mission patterns, innovators are asking God to show them new ways, not necessarily better, but ways that will add another dimension to expand our impact and see churches planted in places where Christ has never been known.

The Risk of Going It Alone

Probably one of the riskiest methods, most fraught with dangers, is the American Christian who visits a Two-Thirds World country, meets a Christian worker and unilaterally begins supporting him or her financially. Without adequate information or background, the naive traveller may give unwisely, destroying the stewardship of a ministry that could operate on its own. Or he may cause jealousy between Christian workers by providing one with money or equipment that the others don't have. Unfortunately sometimes the unwary visitor may be completely fooled by a con artist who fabricates stories of needs and results that never occurred. There are sound reasons why both the national church and the mission agencies discourage Lone Rangers and encourage assistance to come through recognized and acceptable channels.

But now and again it's worth taking the risk to work with a Spirit-directed entrepreneur. Jim Reapsome, veteran mission editor of the *Evangelical Missions Quarterly,* has taken such a risk.

Traveling in a Middle Eastern country, he met Assad (a pseudonym), a courageous Arab Christian who had established a Christian book store and literature ministry in the midst of a hostile Muslim community. Reapsome was impressed that this man was willing to put his life on the line because he recognized the importance of providing Christian literature for the minuscule Christian community and those who were seeking to know more about Christ.

Assad's tiny national corporation needed funds, additional personnel and increased retail space to operate effectively, but had no resources to draw on. Jim took the risk.

Jim explained:

I invited him over here to meet a number of different publishers and Christian friends. He generated a lot of interest and support, but it's strictly on a one-to-one basis where I'm partnering with him because I believe that literature is a key to our Christian presence and witness in the Middle East.

Out of his long years of working with mission leaders, Reapsome knew his partner had to meet the following basic requirements:

1. Integrity. Jim met Assad through the recommendation of a veteran missionary, and spoke to other mission leaders who vouched for Assad's known track record over a number of years.

2. Strategic financial planning. Since this is a business that will have to stand on its own eventually, it was essential that Assad have a realistic budget and projected plans that were sound financially. Reapsome was impressed with the detailed proposal that Assad prepared for the international advisory board he had set up.

3. A broad and strategic vision. It must have long-range potential and not be the dream of one person which will die with him. The literature program was not a one-man show, nor was Assad asking

for items that would enrich him personally. "I stayed with him in his home, and I saw the way the man and his family lives . . . extremely modest," Jim commented. He was impressed with the personal qualities and strengths of Assad which he came to recognize as they spent time in each other's homes.

Reapsome believes personal partnerships can work if the church or individual makes a careful and prayerful analysis. But few have the experience and knowledge of missions that this veteran missiologist has, and most might do better taking advantage of agencies who have such insights and expertise.

Church-to-Church Partnerships

As the baby-boomers become more prominent in the leadership and financial growth of the church, their tendency for individualism and desire to control their own destiny affects even church mission strategies. A study of baby-boomers indicates that they are generally more interested in solving the problems of poverty and injustice close to home than in foreign missions. They are more likely to respond to a person they know than the needs of millions they don't know.

A mission-pastor in a megachurch observes:

We looked at the age group behind our missions program. It's not the forty and under group. They are not interested in missions, nor are they supporting it.

Some churches are finding that forming a partnership with a sister-church in a restricted country is a way to stir up mission interest in the baby-boomer generation and give them opportunity for involvement on a personal level.

Meanwhile several mission agencies have sprung up in the late eighties with a special concern for the Christians in restricted countries and where minority Christians feel isolated and vulnerable.

Issachar, an organization focusing on mission strategies to unreached peoples, established its ENOSIS program as an outgrowth of the Lausanne Congress in Manila in 1989, to develop an international sister-church partnership movement. ENOSIS means to link two parties to form a strong bond.

Issachar believes the problems of access to restricted people, as well as language and cultural barriers, can be counteracted by a link between Western churches and Two-Thirds World churches in those areas. The churches in turn need help with training, materials and finances.

By bringing leaders and laypeople of the two churches together through visits back and forth, it is envisioned that each would learn from and pray for the other. Eventually the two churches would cooperate in an outreach program. The mission experience and vision of a Western church is one of the prime contributions it could make to its sister church. In the meantime, the Western church benefits tremendously from the interaction with Christians who have suffered and lived in a society hostile to Christianity.

In planning to launch such a sister-church program, Reverend Val Hayworth, missions pastor of the Elmbrook Church in Brookfield, Wisconsin, admits one of the motivating factors is to mobilize the younger leaders in the church. "We have identified about twenty families in the fellowship who are influential movers and proving themselves in ministry," Hayworth explains. "We're asking them to consider making a trip to visit the Russian church at their own expense."

Elmbrook Church will provide crosscultural training to prepare the travelers for their visit to the Soviet Union. The process will take a number of years, with five or six annual visits to the sister church. A Soviet church leader will be brought here, also, to spend some time observing the church life at Elmbrook.

Hayworth says:

Our ultimate objective is to hold a cooperative evangelistic thrust after a few years, where the two churches together will target a group. We might provide training for special ministries such as women or children.

But Hayworth and Issachar insist that the relationship is not financially driven. The church is under no financial obligation other than to keep the communication and visitation going. They recognize that there will undoubtedly be requests for financial assistance, and policies need to be agreed upon from the beginning if the partnership is to be successful.

Another sister-church organization, ASSIST (Aid to Special Saints in Strategic Times), founded by award-winning journalist, Dan Wooding, initially targeted a "twinning" relationship with churches in Cuba and Nicaragua. It has also made contacts with churches in such places as Thailand, Myanmar (Burma), and even North Korea.

Founded in 1988, the program encourages correspondence between members of the two churches and sets out careful guidelines in order to avoid misunderstandings or politically sensitive issues.

But ASSIST believes strongly that the Western partner needs to not only pray for the partner church but also supply part of its needs. Churches in Cuba, for example, have almost no access to Christian literature; pastors have few study books. Many churches meet in homes (which have no pews for seating). Pastors have no means of transportation.

ASSIST encourages donors to send money to the mission rather than directly to the sister church. "We don't want them to come to a position where they become spoiled children and expect everything to be provided by the church here," declares a spokesperson. So the organization encourages donors to give to a general fund and seeks to take care of distribution equitably.

Both sister-church programs are convinced that the Western churches benefit from the prayers of their sister church and experience spiritual growth, especially as visitors have the opportunity to see faith and love grow under suffering and persecution. The "hands on" involvement results in greater mission awareness and commitment at home.

Until models have developed and been tested by time, questions as to the effectiveness of this method will continue to be raised, and methods refined.

Will the energy and funds used to develop relationships between bodies of believers actually bring about additional church planting and outreach?

Will the concentrated involvement of the church people and the personal expenses of individual families in travel restrict the broader missions program of the church?

Can a relationship between a materially wealthy Western church and a materially poor Two-Thirds-World church develop without paternalism and a "sugar daddy" complex on one side and envy and dependency on the other?

Or are these questions simply a reflection of our paternalistic attitudes emerging again?

Church-Based Teams

Church-based teams are another innovative way to harness the involvement and interest of a larger percentage of a congregation. Led by a highly committed senior pastor, the church recruits, trains and sends out a team of its own members to a target city or area.

More and more churches seem to want greater control over their missionaries and greater contact with them. The fleeting visit of a missionary making the rounds on furlough makes it difficult for the people in the church to develop a meaningful relationship or a committed prayer base. Church-based teams offer an opportunity to fill both these needs.

With a growing number of countries restricting career missionaries, particularly in Muslim areas, tent-making is one of the few ways to establish a permanent base. But tent-making can be a dangerously lonely ministry when there is no local church or fellowship and no missionary support nearby. Tim Lewis of Frontier Missions says he knows of few independent tent-makers able to stay in Muslim countries more than two years, even when they are relatively successful in terms of ministry.

The church-based team provides close family support, on the field as well as from the home base as the congregation focuses its prayers, gifts and communications on their brothers and sisters on the front line. As one pastor from such a church states, "The whole church is the team."

Sending a church team out together has probably been tried in various degrees of success and failure in past years. But since the late 1980s the idea has developed with more urgency and purpose. The Antioch Network, a loose fellowship of about twenty churches, was incorporated in 1989, to help churches investigate the concept, share vision, success stories and failures.

Antioch Network grew out of the vision of George Miley, former Operation Mobilization director of the Logos and Doulos ships. Interaction with missionaries and local churches resulted in the conviction that fresh, innovative approaches to world evangelization were needed. As a speaker on missions in a wide variety of churches, George found that others were dreaming too, and the idea of church-sponsored teams planting churches among unreached people crystallized.

A church in Austin, Texas (not identified for security reasons), has had a team in the Middle East since 1987. Team members have established legitimate reasons for living in the country. Even while concentrating on language study, they have been able to develop friendships in the community.

On his first visit to research the target community, the pastor and several of his church members were arrested and held for questioning by local police because of contacts they had made.

"I have the impression the Lord allowed that to happen to sensitize us to the dangers and make us more careful in the future," the pastor explains.

The team had been prepared for its ministry through training programs at the church, such as the U.S. Center Prospectives course, and supervised practical work on the church staff. With the pastor's experience fresh in their minds, elaborate security measures were put in place which have added to the feeling of isolation.

However, the church has taken its responsibility to the team seriously. The missions pastor communicates frequently by phone or fax, and he and members of the church visit the team each year. For several years a summer team visited the target city, with a host couple renting an apartment so that relays of church members could stay for a few weeks holiday at reasonable cost. The idea was not to evangelize but to mobilize and maintain the vision, which would naturally drop off in time.

The Texas church has maintained a high rate of interest, with between 30 to 40 per cent of the members financially involved in the project. About 50 per cent of the church's mission budget is dedicated to the team. Even though team members will eventually be self-supporting within the country, travel, medical insurance and other such costs are the church's responsibility.

This church chose to work outside a mission agency partly because no agency was able at the time to incorporate the team concept. Other churches who have sent teams have been able to work through an agency, and one even has a representative on the agency's board to solidify the partnership.

Are the teams successful? Miley says:

> The book hasn't been written yet on how we plant churches in Muslim countries. . . . But our commitment must be to constant innovation in all areas. In order for this to exist there must be tolerance of well-intended failures and we must support persistent champions of innovation.

Church-based teams require the total vision of the senior pastor and the ability to mobilize the congregation's long-term commitment. One danger is that if the pastor leaves the church, the team could be stranded if the successor does not share the vision. Unless a high percentage of the congregation has bought into the vision, many in the congregation will feel left out and frustrated that so much energy in the church is concentrated on one project.

The strategy is costly in time and energy. Though some churches feel they can send their missionaries "cheaper" than through an agency, they must honestly examine the hidden costs of staff time, administration, as well as travel costs for church members who visit the field at their own expense.

But those who have taken the risk and sent out a church-based team have found the benefits deeply gratifying. The atmosphere in the church resembles that of a family where a member is serving overseas. Every letter is avidly shared; personal events and disappointments become intimate matters of prayer. Family members can share failures as well as successes, so if one of the team is homesick or depressed, he or she doesn't fear revealing that to the family at home.

The prayer power is unmatched. Every traditional missionary has some faithful prayer partners in the various churches which support him. But few have the strength of a "Nehemiah group" as one church-based team has. The pastor of this Arizona sending-church writes:

> For several years we have required that every outgoing missionary surround himself or herself with a group of ten praying adults (a couple would have twenty). This Nehemiah Prayer Group covenant to (1) pray regularly, daily, for the specific needs of their missionaries; (2) write regularly, monthly, to keep all parties well informed; (3) foster an ongoing friendship with their missionary through phone calls, care packages and even personal visits when possible, and (4) encourage other Nehemiah Prayer Group members to do the same.

When the first team members on the field decided to stay past their second year so they could solidify their language gains, they wrote back home to the pastor, "Please send us some comfort—send someone from our Nehemiah group to visit."

And after an especially trying time of depression the team member expressed deep gratitude and victory after hearing how the Nehemiah group had prayed for him.

In spite of the tremendous benefits gained by the church, the question still remains, Will these inexperienced and isolated teams be able to hold out in the face of hostility and isolation? And more importantly, will they be able to plant a viable church in a hostile Muslim community?

Tim Lewis voices these grave doubts:

On the field the local [Western] church has very little relevance to the problems of planting churches in Muslim restricted access situations . . . we have learned so much in the eight years of our existence that I really have to say that we're light years ahead of the ability to support and coach a team doing that on the field, over a local church, no matter how committed.

To By-pass or Not to By-pass the Agency

Today's missions committees have become more knowledgeable about missions, and many larger churches have a full-time missions pastor on their staff. They have asked more questions and analyzed the effectiveness of missionaries and their agencies. Generally this has encouraged agencies and missionaries to be more even more accountable and has helped churches to better understand the complexities of the problems and challenged on the field.

But to some extent, it has also created tension between the two entities, sometimes even a "we/they" attitude. Churches want more jurisdiction over the missionaries they support; agencies feel local churches are too demanding and sometimes naive about their expectations. On the whole it has been a healthy, productive tension in the broadest mission partnerships in the world, the local churches and the sending agencies.

However, as the innovative partnerships we've discussed in this chapter indicate, there is a growing trend to by-pass the agency and deal directly with the missionary or the national church on the field. Obviously mission agencies will never disappear in favor of church-based teams, nor will churches give up trying their own innovative approaches. But in every case, the pros and cons have to be carefully analyzed to make sure this is the most effective way to plant the church and develop disciples on any given field.

Advantages of the Local Church-Based Mission Program

1. Many churches desire greater autonomy and ownership of their missionary outreach. They see great advantages in recruiting missionaries whom they know well and who share the same goals and visions. They want the missionaries responsible to them, and they would like to work directly with the national church on the field.

2. When the missionaries are home, they can spend quality time with the local church, developing close relationships. In turn members of the congregation will maintain a personal interest in the missionaries when they return to the field. This gives everyone in the church a greater sense of ownership of the project. Mission giving goes up as a result.

3. Intense, regular, personal prayer support develops. Missionaries can share their intimate problems and their failures as well as successes because of the secure relationships, and they can depend on committed prayer warriors.

4. Communication from the field improves because the missionary or national ministry only has to write to one supporting prayer group.

5. The team or the national ministry has the sense of belonging and being well cared for because the church can concentrate on their needs.

6. Churches involved in direct ministries believe they are saving the agency-cost of servicing the missionary. Some say they save at least 20 per cent by sending the missionary out themselves.

Advantages of the Agency-Based Ministry

1. Most agencies have years of experience in church planting, in the customs and regulations of the country and in how to handle legal matters for the missionaries. They have developed sound missiological principles and a deep understanding of relations with the church.

2. An agency can provide consistent monitoring and supervision of the work on the field and give moral and spiritual support when it is needed.

3. A mission agency's goals and policies remain constant and do not change as readily as a local church's do when leadership changes.

4. Mission agencies have developed networks with others doing similar work around the world. They have been able to exchange ideas, successes and failures.

5. The mission agency staff handles such time-consuming business matters as taxes, receipting, insurance, retirement and so on. It has standard procedures for recruiting and evaluation. These and many other services must be repeated by each individual church which by-passes the agency, putting additional strain on the local staff.

6. Mission agencies have a broader financial base than the local church, enabling them to pool resources. This is especially important for smaller churches which would not be able to support even one missionary fully on their own.

7. By utilizing agencies and sharing in the partial support for various ministries, churches can broaden their mission involvement to meet the interests of everyone in the congregation.

A pastor who is very involved in a church-based team reflects on these tensions. He observes:

I think that both local churches and mission agencies can't quite believe that the other one would be willing to partner in this way. I think we will see in the next two or three years a coming together of mission agencies and local churches on a much stronger basis.

Perhaps these two long-standing bastions of mission work will themselves come up with some innovative partnerships for the twenty-first century.

Chapter 12
Global Glue

Africa used to be a long way from the United States. It took missionaries three weeks by ship to reach South Africa in the early fifties when mission terms were five years long, and no one thought of going home for the funeral of a loved one. But today Africa is just a fax away and you can watch the World Series over CNN in a Nairobi hotel as easily as in New York.

Everywhere you travel somebody speaks English, which is fast becoming the global language. Today there are one billion English-speaking people. That number will increase to one and a half billion by the year 2000.

Telephone, travel, fax, TV, common language, international trade: these help to make up the global glue which pulls us together into Malcolm Muggeridge's "global village."

The Christian church in the West really has little excuse not to know the conditions, stresses and repressions in the rest of the world. And every Two-Thirds World country has Christian leaders who have travelled, studied or attended conferences in other parts of the world.

In this milieu global partnerships make sense, for Christians, above all other groups of people in the world, have a common cause: to spread the message of Christ so that everyone has an opportunity to hear the gospel clearly.

Global partnerships are, understandably, less formal, less organized, less controlled than the relationships between churches or organizations. Global partnerships tend to be very focused, responding to the deep-felt need of the Christian community around the world.

Though the Holy Spirit usually raises up one or two key leaders as catalysts to the vision, the Lord also moves in the hearts of his people so that others in different places and groups sense the urgency at the same time.

The Link with the Unreached World

The concept of "unreached people," first introduced by Ralph Winter and Donald McGavran, has become common to anyone interested or involved in missions today. Defining unreached people as a group bound together by language and customs and in which there is no church able to reproduce itself, mission researchers estimate there are some 2,000 major unreached groups in the world today.

But where are they? Who is working among them? How can they be reached? How can we avoid duplication of efforts? What is the closest group linguistically and culturally to these people? Are there any Christians among them at all?

To answer these and other questions a number of mission research agencies have pooled their resources and opened up their data banks to each other and to agencies and churches who need the information. World-renowned researchers such as Patrick Johnstone (WEC), who wrote *Operation World,* and David Barrett (Southern Baptist Foreign Mission Board), editor of *World Christian Encyclopedia,* are cooperating with researchers at MARC (World Vision), the Global Mapping Project and Adopt-a-People based at the U.S. Center for World Mission in Pasadena.

By making their data bases available to each other, researchers eliminate duplication and make the information available to those who need it.

The Adopt-a-People Clearing House in Pasadena avails itself of this information. They track the unreached people. They determine whether or not anyone is working among them, the status of that penetration and what churches or other organizations, if any, are partnering in the task. Adopt-a-People Clearinghouse makes information available to churches who would like to target a group in a certain country or region.

For example, Westminster Chapel in Bellevue, Washington, wanted to partner with an existing mission agency. They approached SIM, saying virtually, "What can we do? We don't have our own agenda, we just want to help where we can to reach an unreached people."

SIM recommended the Mursi tribe in Ethiopia, an enclave of 6,000 people living in one of the most inaccessible areas of the world. Their territory is surrounded by three rivers with no roads or bridges connecting them to the outside world. The Marxist government hasn't bothered to develop any amenities for the people because of their intertribal wars and endemic cattle raids.

Ethiopian evangelists from another tribe made initial contacts with the people and were able to give SIM missionaries an insight into this animistic tribe. Since cattle are the main source of food and sustenance, the people slaughter one of their stock animals whenever there is trouble in the village. Witch doctors seek spiritual guidance by spreading an animal's intestines on the ground in a special formation. Blood spots on the intestines, for example, indicate there will be a cattle raid in the near future.

SIM accepted Westminster Chapel's offer and invited the church to send a team to investigate the area. In 1986 four members of the church, including the senior pastor, Mark Neuenschwander, visited Ethiopia. Though they could not enter Mursi territory because of the lack of roads and bridges, they met with missionaries and evangelists and saw how the people in the surrounding area live.

At home the congregation carried out a round-the-clock prayer vigil until the team returned, just in time to report at the annual missions conference.

The church agreed to accept the challenge, and they established Operation Reach Task Force as part of their missions committee. It has sent funds to build roads and to provide partial support for two SIM missionaries. The money also helps several Ethiopian evangelists now living in the Mursi area.

Over a four-year period the church has sent six short-term missionaries, primarily to help with building projects. The church receives regular reports which are shared with the whole congregation. News of the first two Mursi converts in 1990 brought great joy.

Task force leader Tom Hodges says, "Besides the Lord, the support from the pulpit is key to the success of this project." He praises the Lord for the enthusiastic support of Westminster Chapel's pastor.

SIM is just one of thirty-eight mission agencies who provide information to the Adopt-a-People Clearing House about groups they have discovered or have started to work in. Along with on-site investigation by missionaries, research groups assist in analyzing and verifying data so that Adopt-a-People can match a church and agency in reaching an unreached group.

One of the goals which grew out of the Unreached People Track at Lausanne II in Manila in 1989 was to research and publish descriptions of the estimated 2,000 major unreached people, and as many as 12,000 smaller unreached groups within these larger ones.

Nothing short of global cooperation and a supernatural commitment to what will often be drudgery and persistence will be able to accomplish this monumental task. No one organization could possibly do it alone; nor will a multiplication of organizations protecting their own turf and information complete the task of world evangelization.

Getting National Churches to Work Together

Mobilizing the local church is an essential part of reaching the world for Christ. In North America mission committees spend many hours figuring out ways to "sell" missions, to involve the congregation, and far too often, how to help the pastor become a world Christian himself. There's no denying the urgency of community needs and the local church's responsibility to do all it can to meet those needs. But the church's imbalance of involvement between local and international concerns is pretty well reflected in the same imbalance in our evening news. Churches in the Two-Thirds World face additional obstacles to cooperation in world evangelization because of lack of information and finances. But in spite of these limitations Two-Thirds World churches are beginning to make great strides in partnering to reach the unreached.

DAWN Ministries, founded by James Montgomery, serves as a catalyst to bring national churches of all persuasions together to understand the needs of the lost and to strategize how to reach them cooperatively. Montgomery describes DAWN's basic premise as "the whole Body of Christ in a whole country beginning to perceive itself as a body and functioning as a body."

For many years Montgomery had studied the problems of lack of cooperation and inability to get churches working together. He recognized that denominational, organizational and policy differences kept churches suspicious and afraid to identify with each other. All too often they'd experienced condemnation and even expulsion if they cooperated across "forbidden lines."

Montgomery concluded, "The realization came somewhere along the line that the way to get the church working together most effectively in a country is to work toward a common goal." DAWN defines that common goal as evangelizing and planting a target number of churches in an entire country by a specified date.

DAWN teams have held seminars in Asia, Africa, Europe, the Middle East and Latin America to mobilize and train church leaders and to help them set joint goals. The churches finance their own programs. "But we help financially with research," says Montgomery, "because it's the information that challenges the church to do something."

The first DAWN program in the Philippines has a goal of 50,000 churches by the year 2000, and at last count was right on target. In El Salvador John Knoxer (as national DAWN leaders who have the burden and vision for national church growth are referred to) Adonai Leiva reports exciting developments there:

It took 100 years to plant the first 3500 churches in El Salvador. With the DAWN project, 1000 more churches have been planted in just the past two years! More and more denominations are setting goals in order to reach the national goal of reaching 35% of the population by the end of this year [1990].

Since Lausanne II, DAWN has received more invitations for seminars than it can handle. The ultimate success, however, will depend on the ability of church leaders in a nation to give up denominational pride and narrow perceptions of cooperation and develop partnerships of trust with other parts of Christ's body in the nation.

Communicating in the Languages of the World

In 1985 the four major Christian radio organizations in the world formed a coalition to make sure that every man, woman and child on Planet Earth can turn on their radio and hear the gospel in a language they can understand.

The agreement drawn up by HCJB, Far Eastern Broadcasting

Company (FEBC), Trans World Radio (TWR) and later ELWA in Liberia revealed as much about their previous relationship as it did about their future goals.

Dr. Ron Cline, president of HCJB, described the agreement, which formed the basis of World by 2000:

1. We will not compete with each other.

Now, you know, we never really officially competed. We at HCJB just used terminology like "the biggest" or "the best" or, sometimes, "We reach 80 percent of the world." And then Paul Freed (of Trans World Radio) would say, "We reach 81 percent of the world." And Bob Bowman (of FEBC) would come up with "82.5 percent of the world." And then, of course, we would revamp our figure to include "83 percent of the world."

Well, we agreed we would not waste our energy on that nonsense.

2. We are not enemies one of the other.

The Christian Church is really active in shooting at each other. Sometimes we're more concerned with the church down the street than with all the sinners that live in between the two churches. We are very much in competition, and we begin to think the other church is the enemy.

In fact, many of you live in parts of the world that, when you line up the good guys and the bad guys, some of you would have a hard time standing beside someone who perhaps was baptized forward instead of backwards, or perhaps beside someone who raises his hands while he sings even when he sings, "I Lift My Hands to Thee." (Some of us bury our hands in our pockets.) Or we get hung up because others use a different translation of a Bible.

We've gotten really confused who the enemy is, and we spend all of our energy fighting each other rather than the real enemy. So our agreement that day included who the enemy was, and it was not one of us.

3. We need to do what we say we are doing.

We have glorious statements in all of our publicity as to what we are doing and who we are. HCJB's statement, for example, says "to communicate the gospel to all the nations." But we were not doing that.

Now, we were sending out wonderful letters with wonderful stories and receiving lots of money, but we were not doing what we said we were doing.

4. We will start trusting each other.

We decided we were not going to try to earn that trust. We were just going to start trusting each other. We weren't going to sit back and say, "Well, when you stop doing this and when you make this right and when this changes and when that changes, then we can start. . . ." No. That day—September 10, 1985—we went out of an office saying, "From this point on, we will trust one another."

From that, a number of things have happened.[1]

As a result, the four organizations set up a small research office at the U.S. Center in Pasadena to pool information rather than harboring it. The goal is to avoid duplication and to work with others who have a vision for evangelizing each of the different language groups. Those involved in radio recognize that cooperation with local evangelists, churches and other organizations is far more effective in establishing and discipling new converts than trying to do it by radio alone.

Since 1985 the coalition has added fourteen major languages (which have one million or more speakers) of the sixty-three languages targeted by the turn of the century. But according to Phil Sandahl, director of the World by 2000 office, "It's like shooting at a moving target."

The four broadcasters are covering approximately 130 major languages, but the number of people groups of a million or more is increasing each year. According to Sandahl, they would have to see

a 10 per cent annual growth in the number of languages needed to
be added to make the goal. He said:

> We've never grown that fast in our history. The other thing is
> that the further down the scale you get, each one becomes more
> difficult than the one before, because the resources are scarcer
> and the numbers [of people who can work in that language] get
> smaller.

But the radio partnership, whose combined signals can actually
reach every place on earth, according to Ron Cline, is producing
more than new languages. There's a new spirit of cooperation and
brotherly love, of unity and helpfulness. Broadcasters not only
share information but technology and personnel.

When Radio ELWA in Liberia had another language they wanted to put on the air, they needed $25,000 to launch the project. Just
at that time a donor approached Ron Cline of HCJB saying he
wanted to help put a new language on the air. When Cline learned
the donor wanted to give $25,000, he gave him ELWA's name and
address and told him to send it to them. With such a spirit of
partnership, adding fifty more languages by the year 2000 might be
easier than we think.

Mobilizing the World Body

In 1948 the World Council of Churches was formed to call churches
to the "goal of visible church unity in one faith and one eucharistic
fellowship," desiring to become the body that would bring the
church around the world into oneness for all the world to see. Some
350 churches from over 100 countries banded together to advance
the cause of Christian unity.

But to most evangelicals the Confession adopted by the WCC
lacked allegiance to such vital issues as the Scripture as the standard of authority and the atonement provided through Christ for
any who would enter his Kingdom.

The World Evangelical Fellowship, representing more than 100 million Christians around the world, serves as the evangelical counterpart to the WCC. Through its national chapters around the world, it provides a voice and visibility to evangelicals within the nation. Though each evangelical fellowship is a loose association of churches and parachurch organizations, many have partnered in concrete ways to provide training, research and relief and development within their own countries. The Nairobi Graduate School of Theology, for example, is a project of the Association of Evangelicals of Africa and Madagascar and provides post-graduate seminary training of the highest quality for students from all over English-speaking Africa.

Lausanne Committee for World Evangelization

In July 1974 a gathering of almost 3,000 Christians from more than 140 countries in Lausanne, Switzerland, became a watershed for world evangelization and the beginning of a movement that has influenced growth and development in the church ever since.

The Congress, born out of Billy Graham's vision, brought participants from remote areas of the Two-Thirds World: pastors from African churches; evangelists from Latin America; Bible teachers from Singapore, the largest gathering of Two-Thirds World Christian leaders up to that time.

The call was to "Let the Earth Hear His Voice," as participants were inspired by spiritual giants of the day like Donald McGavran, Francis Schaeffer, Byang Kato and Festo Kivengere (both from Africa).

Unintentionally, the Lausanne Congress became a movement to continue the momentum of evangelistic fervor and, through its various committees, to deal with broad issues facing the church around the world.

In 1989 the Lausanne Committee, under the leadership of Thomas Wang, sponsored another major congress in Manila, this time with over 4,000 participants. In the fifteen years between congresses, many of the partnerships we've discussed were formed, and relationships between Western and Two-Thirds World leaders became more equal and complementary.

As we've noted earlier, these international forums are invaluable to surface issues and allow interaction on all sides. The long-term value may not be seen immediately, but history has demonstrated that they affect the direction of the Church. Though on a far more critical level, the participants at Nicaea in A.D. 325 could not have perceived the importance of their decisions. In fact, the Nicene Creed used in the Church today was only officially accepted in A.D. 381, fifty-six years after it was formulated.

Lausanne's ultimate effect on the unity and vigor of the world church may not be fully understood for years to come, but it has certainly functioned as part of that global glue which has brought church leaders face to face with each other and helped them to understand the victories and problems that they each face.

Chapter 13

Into the Next Century

L ausanne II participants heard a lot about the goal of world evangelization by the year 2000. The challenge to mobilize Christians to help evangelize the world by the turn of the millennium was repeated over and over. The following opening plenary message emphasized the need for partnership in the global task:

The dawn of partnership with mission movements around the world has become at least mid-morning of a new day in Christianity; a day in which the responsibility for world evangelization is being taken up by the "whole body of Christ." More Christians from more countries are seeking to fulfill the Great Commission than at any time in history. The internationalization of missions is the great new fact of our time. Our challenge is to encourage these new world evangelization initiatives from Africa, Asia and Latin America which at the present rate will place more than 100,000 missionaries in the field by the year 2000.

But not only that, we are challenged by the need to unleash all the forces within the Church in this mobilization. Particularly, we need to see women, young people and lay people within our churches renewed, moved into action and growing as they discover and fulfill their role in world evangelization.

Thus the vision of A.D. 2000 was once again presented to the leaders of the Church around the world. The burden had been articulated by Thomas Wang, international director of the Lausanne Committee, two years earlier in an article in *World Evangelization* titled "By the Year 2000: Is God Trying to Tell Us Something?"

Wang pointed to many bold evangelism thrusts in recent years both among the non-charismatics and charismatics and even Catholics. He quoted missiologist Ralph Winter's conviction that cooperative mission effort can bring about world evangelization as follows:

We believe there are ample evangelical resources in the world community (i.e., 147 congregations per group to be reached!) to make a serious attempt to plant the church within every people by the year 2000, and that such a goal for the year 2000 is therefore a reasonable goal to work and pray for.

But though there have been more than 700 plans of world evangelization throughout the history of the church, most of them in the past have fizzled out. One of the major reasons for the failure has been lack of clear objectives and structure to deal with the obstacles realistically. Another has been the lack of faith and apathy of Christians in the churches. With the failures of the past in mind, and the potential for the future challenging his vision, Wang asked, "What is God trying to say to us?"

So positive was the response to his article that Wang asked the Lausanne Executive Committee to take up the A.D. 2000 leadership and zero in on focused and cooperative world evangelism, setting the year 2000 as a target to work toward. But for various reasons the Lausanne Executive Committee declined to take up the challenge.

In January 1989, over 300 church and mission leaders gathered for the Global Consultation for World Evangelization by A.D. 2000 and Beyond in Singapore. They considered realistically how to cooperate and implement the independent plans already conceived by many of their organizations and to consider what steps, if any, could be taken to formalize the movement so that the impetus would not be lost, as it was in the 1890s.

Though GCOWE participants could not agree on how to structure the A.D. 2000 Movement (some felt another world organization would be redundant; others questioned a Catholic presence in the planning), they did accept the Great Commission Manifesto (see appendix 3) which reads in part:

> We see afresh that cooperation and partnership are absolute necessities if the Great Commission is going to be fulfilled by the year 2000. For the sake of those who are lost and eternally separated from God, we have dared to pray and dream of what might happen if appropriate autonomy of churches and ministries could be balanced with significant partnership.

Yet so urgent were the voices of those who wanted to see the A.D. 2000 Movement be a uniting and motivating force for world evangelization that they would not let the concept die. When the members of the advisory committee of GCOWE II were asked about continuation of the vision, the vast majority were positive.

Lausanne II invited Luis Bush and Bill O'Brien (of the Southern Baptist Foreign Mission Board) to take responsibility for the A.D. 2000 track and Thomas Wang to do a plenary presentation at the Congress, and as a result one of the twelve major points of the Manila Manifesto endorsed the A.D. 2000 vision.

The new international director of Lausanne, Tom Houston, joined his voice with Thomas Wang to explain their relationship:

> The vision of the A.D. 2000 Movement is bold and wide ranging.

It hopes to inspire national A.D. 2000 Consultations and Task Forces in 150 countries by 1993. It hopes in each country to infect with their enthusiasm leaders of churches, seminaries, missions and other Christian organizations, lay men, women and young people. A.D. 2000 wants to be a voice to awaken the churches to the urgency of the task and the conviction that it can be done by A.D. 2000.[1]

To assure the leaders of the church that there is no spirit of competition or duplication between the two groups, the writers close the article with these words of partnership:

The leaders of the A.D. 2000 Movement and those of LCWE will be in regular contact with each other both at the international and the national level. They see their efforts as complementary in the task of world evangelization and will work at ensuring that there is no duplication or fragmentation of effort.[2]

While this statement is commendable, grassroots leadership around the world still questions the lack of unity this represents, as well as the need for two such organizations.

Breaking the Logjam

The Iguazu Falls forms a natural frontier between Brazil and Argentina. A short distance below the falls, trees are cut for lumber and the trunks thrown into the river to flow down to a sawmill. During the dry season, the river often runs lower than normal and logjams arise frequently. Tree trunks point in a hundred and one different directions, as if each log has a mind of its own with no common sense of direction. As the river rises, the logs begin to point in the same direction until, finally, the logjam is broken and the logs flow down together to fulfill their common mission.

Water is often used in the Scriptures to symbolize the Holy Spirit. The logjam of the A.D. 2000 Movement gradually broke up as the Holy Spirit moved upon planners, and church and mission leaders. These Christians were infused with a new breath of excitement and expectancy, a new sense of cooperation and partnership to the Christian church around the world. It's as though God's word to Isaiah was being fulfilled once again when he said, "See, I am doing a new thing! Now it springs up; do you not perceive it? I am making a way in the desert and streams in the wasteland" (Is 43:19).

Even before the planning committee could finalize its purpose and plan its milestones, the Costa Rican evangelicals demonstrated what could happen through the A.D. 2000 Movement as God worked. The Costa Rican secular press warned its readers of the growth of the "Protestant sects," explaining that the church had grown from 10 per cent in 1980 to 18 per cent in 1989.

While non-evangelicals may be uneasy about the rapid growth of the evangelical church, Costa Rican Christians rejoice in what God is doing, and recognize their responsibility in world evangelism. In April 1990, hundreds of Costa Ricans attended "Alcance 2000" (Outreach 2000), a missions congress which grew out of the COMIBAM congress in 1987 in São Paulo and the Global Congress on World Evangelism in Singapore in January 1989.

The declaration of Alcance 2000 in Costa Rica affirmed the commitment to consider the year 2000 as a strategic date for the evangelization of Costa Rica and the world. Pastors and denominational leaders committed themselves to the goal of sending between 200 and 500 missionaries to start a church-planting movement among thirty to fifty unreached people groups by the year 2000.

The participants considered this the Costa Rican church's proportional part of the challenge of reaching the estimated 12,000 (subcultures of the 2,000 peoples) remaining unreached-people groups in the world. This goal was based on the percentage of evangelicals in Costa Rica in relation to the total number of evangelicals in the world, setting a model for other national churches to follow.

Not satisfied with simply laying plans, the participants set in motion the machinery to establish the first Costa Rican interdenominational mission agency and appointed leaders to make it happen.

Other such consultations have been held in Ghana, Nigeria, India, Argentina, Colombia and among Chinese Christian leaders of North America. One of the goals of the A.D. 2000 Movement is to encourage such national consultations in as many countries as possible so that national leaders can receive a vision for the unreached and work together to reach them.

Why Target A.D. 2000?

But why all the fuss about the year 2000? Aren't we getting dangerously close to setting a date for the Lord's return by targeting the year 2000 to reach the world for Christ? The A.D. 2000 Movement does not attach any eschatological meaning to the year 2000. But it realizes that it is a powerful target which can help to accelerate the church's effort for evangelism.

The Bible doesn't teach that everyone will be saved, but it does say there will be representatives from every people, tribe and nation. For the A.D. 2000 planners, world evangelization will be complete when a mission-minded church-planting movement has been established within every unreached people and city so that all peoples might have a valid opportunity to experience the love, truth and saving power of Jesus Christ. They believe this can be done by the turn of the millennium.

Thomas Wang, chairman of the A.D. 2000 Movement, is convinced the possibility is finally in sight. In an editorial in the first issues of the *A.D. 2000 and Beyond* magazine he wrote:

Today the Spirit of God is at work in a more powerful and universal manner. Different denominations, gospel and mission groups are mounting no less than 200 global projects on world evangelization with most of them taking the year 2000 as their target. If the voices of the last century were solos and duets, we are now hearing the magnificent prelude of a gigantic worldwide chorale swelling up in a heart-warming crescendo. God must have waited a long time for this sweet music.

Is This Just Another International Organization?

The A.D. 2000 committee is firmly committed to the principle that this is a movement, and unlike an institution, is not meant for permanent existence. It sees the value of its functions until the year 2000.

Leaders of the movement work out of their own offices with the approval and blessing of the ministries they serve. Furthermore, rather than setting up committees and offices around the world, A.D. 2000 desires to motivate men and women church leaders through existing networks by inspiring vision through consultations, prayer efforts and written materials.

In order to enhance as many leadership networks as possible, track coordinators have been appointed to work with various interest groups in the church such as those concerned with church planting, unreached groups, women, youth and so on. Track leaders encourage cooperative relationships with existing movements and networks that will result in coordinated efforts to evangelize unreached peoples and urban centers. For example, in countries where the DAWN Movement is active, A.D. 2000 track leaders gladly join hands while also providing vision for world evangelization beyond the borders of that country.

What Major Milestones Lie Ahead?

The A.D. 2000 Planning Committee set ambitious milestones, convinced of God's direction in the movement and that the worldwide church was equipped to fulfill the task. The movement set plans in motion to mobilize 100,000 intercessors for world evangelism and concerts of prayer in 1,000 cities. Transmitting information and inspiration along thousands of existing networks, the movement

leaders visualize an accelerating momentum of world evangelization.

As churches and parachurch organizations join in partnership,
the possibilities for reaching their goals increase. Before the middle
of the nineties, they are praying that 2,000 people groups, 1,000
unevangelized cities and the 50 least-evangelized countries will have
been adopted.

The Global Congress on World Evangelism in 1994 is to serve
as a mid-decade evaluation of progress and a mid-course adjustment of where to go from there in order to reach the target by A.D.
2000. Hopefully the church will not have to admit defeat as it did
in 1895 before the turn of the last century. Another congress to
celebrate the victories and rejoice in the growth of the church in this
final decade of the millennium is envisioned for the year 2000. Only
as those of us in Christ, who preach a Christ-centered message
based on the Word of God, partner together with each other under
the leadership of the Holy Spirit can these dreams be realized.

We don't need to compete. There's more than enough work for
everybody. In Luke 5 the disciples had been out all night fishing
without catching anything. When they did as Jesus said, ". . . they
caught such a large number of fish that their nets began to break.
So they signaled their partners in the other boat to come and help
them, and they came and filled both boats so full that they began
to sink" (Lk 5:6-7).

There are enough fish for everyone. Let us put worldly competition behind us. Let us not fish alone. Let us do as Jesus says and
call our partners in the other boat to come and help us.

Chapter 14

Teaming Up to Give

When Dr. Chris Marantika, president of the Evangelical Theological Seminary of Indonesia (ETSI), talks about church planting, he can't contain his excitement. He's seen more than 600 churches planted by the students of the seminary, and he's convinced that "Muslims are winnable."

While many Two-Thirds World Christian leaders share his optimism for victory, so many American Christians don't know there's a war on or that it's winnable. Yet we control the financial ammunition to equip the troops and keep them moving.

We have spoken in this book of the problem of the power and dominance of money and the obstacle this is to true partnership. Yet, it cannot be denied that money is an important weapon in the battle for the world's soul. Scripture clearly teaches us that we are to use it in kingdom warfare. While 80 per cent of the world's Christian money is in North America, the average Christian gives away only 2.5 per cent of his income (compared with 1.7 per cent for the non-Christian!). And of that only 4 per cent is going to reach the billions of unreached people in the Two-Thirds World.

In the next twenty years an estimated $6.8 trillion will be transferred from the estates of the post-World War 2 entrepreneurs to those left behind. As Greg Ring, president of the Dallas Seminary Foundation, says, "The race is on as to who will get this money—their children, the I.R.S., or charity."

Ring estimates that if only 5 per cent of wealthy people in America are Christian (a conservative figure since the Gallup poll indicates that 30 per cent claim to be born again) $185 billion stands ready to be passed down. Almost by default, as much as two-thirds could be lost to income and state taxes because so few people do any creative planning. The balance will pass on to today's baby-boomers who, studies show, are generally not interested in foreign missions.

Ring is concerned that so many Christians know nothing of sacrificial giving, that wealthy Christians know little about tax-wise giving and that those who inherit the money have little concern about providing ammunition for the spiritual battles in the Two-Thirds World.

Wealthy Christians Struggle
Most Christians want to use their money wisely, particularly those who have spent their lives to build a successful business and make smart investments. Yet when it comes to giving to the work of God, they often don't know where to give, and Christian organizations don't know how to challenge them. Unfortunately, their pastors may not help them give wisely to missions because some pastors are jealous for the needs of their own churches. Bombarded by appeals from every side, these Christians find it difficult to discern what will make a significant impact for God.

The story is told of a wealthy donor who makes his contributions at the end of the year. He spreads the various appeals around on his desk and across the floor, trying to decide to which he should respond. One year he wrote a check for all 129 requests but, he confessed, "This is the worst job in the world. I have absolutely no idea who to give to."

Not only do wealthy Christians not know where to give, but they don't realize when they have enough. Ron Blue, author of *Mastering Your Money,* says that very few well-to-do Christians know the finish line. "If you have enough to be financially independent, pay off your debts, send kids to college, why do you need more?" Over-accumulation is a driving force in American society as we try to fulfill our basic needs of security and significance. But Blue contends that, with careful planning, a person can know when he has enough and be free to give the rest to God, who "owns it all" in the first place.

To counteract this malaise and help Christians, especially those who have the responsibility for large sums of money, several organizations are offering to partner with them in helping them to become wise stewards.

Learning to Give
Helping wealthy Christians give wisely is a partnership that excites Hugh Maclellan, Jr., president of the Maclellan Foundation. Maclellan says:

There are so many wealthy Americans. We know one man who is worth $100 million, another $300 million. The problem is they're not connected to anything. We need to build a base of experts so that when they call and say, "I need help. I want to give in the area of Africa? Whom should I call?" we can direct them to someone.

In February 1989 the Maclellan Foundation joined with the William Johnson Foundation to invite over 100 major donors to a conference at the Johnson-owned Ritz Carlton Hotel in Atlanta. Their purpose was to broaden the vision of these Christians, expose them to different organizations, and help them "give more and give more strategically."

A sense of excitement permeated the discussions as participants listened, not only to knowledgeable mission experts draw the big picture of what is happening in the Two-Thirds World, but to financial planners who helped them to see how they could be significantly involved. One man's evaluation was, "I've been giving a million dollars away, and I see now that I need to be giving $5 million a year."

Later that year, twenty-five evangelical foundations met together to discover ways in which they could team up to be more effective in their giving ministry. Pat MacMillan, a financial consultant for both Christian and secular organizations, challenged the foundation leaders on the power of partnerships. "You cannot do it alone," he urged. "That is a thread woven through the entire Bible. God's work is a team sport." He quoted S. D. Gordon who said:

> Cooperation increases efficiency in amazing proportions. Two working together in perfect agreement have five fold the efficiency of the same two working separately. The united church would be an unconquerable church, but the moment cooperation is sacrificed as essential, real power is at the disappearing point.

Like mission organizations, foundations too have unique strengths which can complement the effectiveness of another foundation. Some have broad access to ministries overseas and have researched the effectiveness of organizations; others have wide contacts in various strata of society.

As a result of this meeting, one foundation was able to re-evaluate its giving and increase it from $700,000 a year to $1.5 million. The director was able to get background information about an organization whose proposal his board was considering from other foundations who had already assisted them. A few months after the conference, he and the head of another large foundation met together with ministry leaders to consider joint funding of a major project. The network is already in place to enable foundations to assist each other in the awesome task of stewardship of millions of dollars of God's money.

The Maclellan Foundation

Hugh Maclellan, Jr., has been one of the major architects of partnering with people of means to enable them to give more and give more strategically.

"I feel bad when I see Christians giving millions of dollars for the arts and civic work," he confided, "when there's a winnable war out there they could be involved in."

The Maclellan Foundation was established in 1952 by the Maclellan family. Robert Maclellan founded the Provident Insurance Company more than 100 years ago. Provident now employs more than 5,000 people nationwide and is the number one company in disability insurance.

In 1887 Robert had come down to Chattanooga from Canada to buy the business for $1,000. While he was completing the transaction, he learned that his daughter back in Canada had died. The family still has the letter he wrote his wife reflecting his deep confidence in his sovereign Lord.

In the first year Robert Maclellan didn't make enough profit to pay himself and the other members of the family who worked with him a salary. Today the company has assets of $14 billion and the foundation, established through personal funds of family members, now gives away about $11.5 million annually.

In 1952 Hugh Maclellan, Sr., who was then president, and his sister Dora established the Maclellan Foundation. One of the senior Maclellan's favorite projects has been right in Chattanooga, where he helped fund a Christian drug abuse program called "Stay Straight," which reaches more than 34,000 kids in the city and county schools. It is now being piloted in ten other cities.

Though retired for more than thirteen years, Maclellan still comes to the office each day and is deeply immersed in the outreach of the foundation. He stays in touch with the world through his wide reading and the many representatives of Christian ministries who come to see him.

Hugh Jr. remembers his Aunt Dora as a little old lady full of vinegar, enthusiasm and energy. For fifty years she taught the same group of women in her Sunday-school class, known as "Aunt Dora's Girls." She was the driving force behind the foundation. Her letter (part of which follows) to the trustees of the Maclellan Foundation in which she explains her will is read annually to the board to remind them of their purpose:

As we go back for generations, the foundation of the Maclellan family has been truly Christian. It is the most valuable heritage we have to pass on to future leaders who are ministering under this name.

Because of this Christian background and training, my own Christian experience has been so precious to me. I long to use my means in a way that will give this privilege to others.

For this reason (more than because it is a "duty" which every Christian should assume), I have had pleasure in supporting Christ's Kingdom on earth.

Her letter goes on to encourage the trustees always to remember the Christian faith upon which the foundation was built.

It is not my wish to make rigid and unchangeable suggestions regarding my estate, but to apply the general principles of encouraging truly Christian causes.

For more than twenty years after she and the other family members had invested their wealth in the foundation, Aunt Dora continued to experience the "pleasure" of supporting God's work before God called her home.

A New Vision for Givers
The man upon whom this awesome mantle of responsibility has

fallen grew up in an environment of controlled wealth and the assumption that giving to God's work was a natural outcome of God's material blessing. Though Hugh Maclellan, Jr., grew up in a Christian home, he admits that he was not discipled until he was thirty years old. But even back then he was giving 20-25 per cent of his money away. He was impressed with people like J. C. Penney who gave 90 per cent away. Today Hugh and his wife give a minimum of 70 per cent to evangelical causes.

"That's not sacrificial at all," says Maclellan. "My fellow Christian in the church who earns $20,000 and gives 10% is much more sacrificial than we are." Maclellan admits that the discipline of giving this amount is a strain. He says:

> But what it's done is that it's kept us, and rightfully so, from ever owning anything. We own no boats, we own no second homes. We just own a house and two cars. We don't take expensive vacations. We've had to maintain a balance in our expenditures in order to give away 70%. And we learned a long time ago that if you own anything, you spend all your time fixing it.

Hugh was able to use a tax law that allowed him to take the full 70 per cent as a deduction. And part of his desire to partner with Christians of means is to encourage them to find ways to plan their investments and giving wisely. He recommends:

> Don't go to your typical lawyer or accountant because they'll try to sell you off of giving to charity. Go to a Christian financial counselor who will help you give more aggressively to the Lord for stewardship and show you how to do this.

Stepping Out into the World

The Maclellan Foundation began seriously funding overseas ministries in the mid-70s. Leighton Ford had invited Hugh Jr. to attend a Lausanne Executive Committee where for the first time Hugh met some of the top Two-Thirds World leaders and learned of the tremendous impact these nationals have in their countries and the financial limitations they work under.

As the desire to make an impact for God around the world grew, Maclellan began to feel he could accomplish more if he left the leadership of Provident Insurance and concentrated on the work of the foundation. He admits: "Actually, God wanted me to get out five years earlier, but I was afraid to step out of my position. Maybe it was due to the power of prestige and position. So God literally kicked me out."

When the company experienced a serious financial reversal, the board fired the management and suggested that Hugh take a board position as chairman of the executive committee. It was a traumatic experience, but Hugh admits he is far more effective on the board, and, above all, he now has time for his first love.

Maclellan started to take some "vision trips" overseas where he met humble, single-minded servants of God seeking to do his will. "For the first time I saw that giving my money to nationals would go much further in winning people to Christ and discipling them than here in the United States," he says. He encourages prospective donors to go overseas themselves and "kick the tires." In fact, in recent years Maclellan has taken every opportunity to help broaden the vision and expose Christians of means to different organizations.

The foundation has very clear parameters for its giving but, even with its relatively large resources, it cannot do the job alone. Its purpose is not to direct gifts to its own causes, but to help people get a bigger vision and learn how to make the greatest impact for God.

Since the mid-70s, the Maclellan Foundation has formed financial partnerships with hundreds of ministries around the world. Major evangelical movements, such as the Lausanne Committee and the World Evangelical Fellowship, as well as smaller missions and individual projects, have benefitted from its grants.

In recent years, however, the foundation has become more pro-active, researching where the most vital outreach is taking place and where its gifts can be used in a multiplying effect. The foundation has singled out experts on various aspects of mission work, inviting them to speak to the trustees and calling them when they need background information. As they listen over and over to reports from people who come for interviews, they ask themselves, "Where is the Holy Spirit moving today in the world?"

A Case Study for Strategic Giving

On the basis of reports from a number of organizations, the foundation concluded that the spiritual hunger of the people of the Soviet Union, and the lack of Christian materials for the 15,000 churches there, was a strategic need.

A number of well-organized and well-staffed mission agencies were available to move into this program and had already begun to restructure their organizations to take advantage of the open doors in the U.S.S.R.

The foundation began looking for people to inform them of how to be effective in giving to the Soviet Union. They are well aware that money given at the wrong time or for the wrong purposes can hinder rather than help a work.

As Hugh Maclellan and others on his staff began calling on as many agencies involved in Eastern Europe as possible, the names of certain knowledgeable people emerged over and over. From this list of names they selected eight experts and interviewed each one. They wanted to know exactly what was going on, who was doing what, what's working and what's needed.

All of the experts underlined the need for literature. Dr. Joseph Tson, head of the Romanian Missionary Society, summarized this urgency, "Whoever is willing to spend the money to get their literature in will set the theological direction of the church for the next one hundred years."

Daily newspaper articles and Christian agency reports on Eastern

Europe and Russia verified the fact that this region would stay open
and be accessible to the gospel for at least two years. At the end
of their research, the foundation felt confident that the potential for
leveraging their funds to make a significant impact for Christ was
possible. In order to harness the giving of other Christians, a consultant suggested a national media campaign to awaken Christians
in America to become involved by:

☐ contributing as many dollars to buy Bibles as the number of
Bibles American Christians have in their homes;

☐ encouraging American churches to equip Russian churches with
a pastor's library, and materials for Sunday-school, evangelism and
discipleship training.

This in turn will supply a ripple effect as the church becomes a
training and lending center for other churches in the area. With this
basic strategy in place, the Maclellan Foundation agreed to partner
with the Slavic Gospel Mission, which they felt had the best contacts and programs for promoting literature and training of Russian Christians; with the Romanian Missionary Society, which was
best prepared to move into that country with literature and lead-
ership-training material; and with Campus Crusade for Christ,
which has good inroads into the academic/intellectual segment of
Russia, and an effective evangelism training for pastors and lay
people. Because of the rapidity of change taking place in the Soviet
Union and Eastern Europe, the foundation chose to limit all giving
to one-year grants with possibilities of renewals.

The following model demonstrates the basic principles which
guide the Maclellan Foundation in granting funds.

1. Ask the questions: Where is the Holy Spirit moving? What are
the most important needs to be met? Are they reaching the unreached or just doing maintenance work? Are the leaders winners,
not losers? (That is, are they godly, humble, teachable, innovative,
with clear purpose and strategy, willing to be held accountable,
cost-effective and capable of being self-perpetuating?)

2. Get into a pro-active stance. Don't just give to requests that come in, but research, travel and call experts to find out the real situation.

3. Get a sense of urgency. One of the greatest needs is funding the kingdom. God can compound your talents and money more than you can.

4. Be an initiator by providing seed money for strategic projects and funds to be an agent of change.

Planned Stewardship

While the Maclellan Foundation primarily partners financially with evangelical ministries around the world, it has a growing vision to help wealthy Christians recognize the need for better stewardship and to know where to give. The "how" falls into the bailiwick of Christian financial planners. A recent California newspaper article warned its readers to beware of religious financial planners, implying that they try to rob little old ladies of their hard-earned savings.

In actuality, financial planners associated with respected Christian organizations can help Christians of even moderate means wisely plan for their future and implement good stewardship principles. But Greg Ring of the Dallas Seminary Foundation believes that people who have the financial resources to give beyond the ordinary, may need more than ordinary financial planning. Coming out of a for-profit background in charitable estate-planning, Ring became concerned that he was spending his life doing good things, like gaining funding for symphony halls, which had no eternal value. He recalls:

I woke up one morning after working with a particularly crotchety elderly businessman and wrote in my prayer journal, "The greatest tragedy that can happen to a Christian is to wake up gray-haired and wrinkled, at the end of a life irrevocably spent in temporal whims and stand before Christ bankrupt for eternity." My wife and I started praying about a change.

In 1982 he approached Dallas Seminary with the idea of offering to help well-to-do Christians with counselling and assistance to meet their stewardship objectives. At a time when tremendous intergenerational transfer of wealth is taking place, Ring believes creative charitable planning can have a great impact, not only in helping clients, but in helping ministries that need new sources of funding for the opportunities before them.

Initially the foundation focused primarily on estate planning, but Ring observed that many people were happy to give their money away when they could no longer use it. "I would like to see them have the joy of giving now," he explains.

Ring recognized that many entrepreneurs faced extraordinary taxes when they decided to sell their businesses. "A man who owns a company can pay 28% income tax, and 55% estate taxes when he dies. This simply immobilizes him." In 1987 Ring assembled a team of highly qualified planners with a variety of technical skills and experience to establish Dallas Seminary Foundation, which works with donors and prospective donors of Christian ministries. The service of the foundation revolves around the creative application of charitable planning concepts to enable Christians to meet their objectives for themselves and their families, increase their giving to the Lord's work, and reduce income and estate taxes.

With proper prior planning, the assets from the sale of a business can be salvaged for kingdom use, and retirees and heirs can still benefit from the investment. For many this has meant a "second life impact." Because of God's material blessings, they now can invest time in ministry, take vision trips, and share their experience and expertise with those who need it. God's people are having fun giving away their funds!

For the Person on the Street

Most of us reading this book can't identify with the problems and responsibilities of the wealthy. But our obligation to partner financially is no less. God has called us to be stewards of what he has given us, and he expects us to be faithful in the little things. The following guidelines for giving speak to us all:

1. We are all going to stand before the Lord to be accountable for how we used the money he has entrusted to us. While we have no right to judge how others spend their money, we are responsible for the choices we make. Ron Blue reminds us of the awesome truth that "every spending decision is a spiritual decision," because they are all God's resources.

2. We must all be wise in the way we use our money for the Lord's work. We may not be able to do the research the Maclellan Foundation did for the project in the Soviet Union, but we can keep abreast of what is happening around the world. Rather than complaining about "junk mail" we ought to read it.

Research tells us that mission articles are the least read in Christian magazines. Publishers say, "Mission books don't sell." When a missionary speaker is announced at church, attendance goes down.

Mission communicators may certainly be at fault, but that does not relieve us of the responsibility to know where God's money is needed and how effectively it is being used. We ought to expect and require letters and reports from those with whom we are partnering so that we know they are using our funds wisely. Information is the fuel of prayer, and prayer is the tool of wisdom. Whether we give $5 or $5 million, it can be wasted and useless if we are not directed by the Holy Spirit and praying that he will make it an effective weapon to build his church.

3. Even Christians with moderate means ought to think about planned giving and how to utilize their resources for God's work after death.

A moderately wealthy widow grieves over the waywardness of her two sons who refuse to have anything to do with the Lord. Instead they have become extremely successful in their careers and are busy collecting the toys that make men boys. She lives frugally and gives generously, but she refuses to draw up a will. Unless she can be convinced of the folly of this course, one day her children will inherit what's left after taxes, and the Lord's army will never have the equipment she could have provided. The burden Hugh Maclellan and Greg Ring have to help wealthy Christians give wisely, joyfully, obediently and timely is the very burden God has for each one of us. He's ready to send his army on the march, and they may just be waiting for our equipment to arrive.

Chapter 15

The Cords of Victory

B y now anyone involved in missions will have realized that partnership is a major issue. The task of world evangelization will most likely be fulfilled when we join our resources and personnel, eliminate duplication and competition, and let God's holy synergism work through partnerships. It is not only the mission agencies and national ministries around the world who need to understand partnership, but those interested in serving crossculturally, missions committees, church leaders and donors.

Those who respond to God's call to service, whether as a career missionary or for a short-term experience, want to use their gifts in the most effective and far-reaching way they can. Using those gifts in a ministry that partners with others can maximize their impact and make their ministry transferable.

Members of mission committees and church leaders take their responsibility to use the funds entrusted into their care seriously. Taking the pulse of partnership helps to evaluate whether the organizations they are supporting are keeping up with this growing trend in missions.

Individuals and foundations want to leverage their funds, investing in ministries that multiply and grow effectively. Knowing the partnership track record of an organization is one way to "give more strategically."

You Can't Take Partnership for Granted

Perhaps our encouraging models of partnership have lulled us into a comfortable sense of satisfaction that the church and missions are at last getting their act together and are right in line with the popular trends of international cooperation and partnership. But you don't have to look too far to know that's not always the case. For example, a British metallurgist accepted a teaching position at a large midwestern university in the U.S.A. a number of years ago. Having come from conservative England where one's personal faith is a very private matter, especially on a university campus, he was impressed with the open influence of Christianity and the many opportunities offered to students. Of course, the Christian community saw the popular and highly respected Christian professor as a feather in its cap.

But whose cap? To his dismay, the professor learned there were twenty-nine Christian organizations on campus, each vying for his presence on their board or program. And it soon became clear that if he joined one, he could not be part of the others.

Even more serious, the professor sensed that each organization was competing for the attention of the students, who themselves were confused about the array of choices and the lack of cooperation between the Christian organizations.

It's not that the leaders of these groups didn't love and appreciate each other, or even that they disagreed with each other's teachings. But each group had its own staff, financial policies, style of ministry and constituency back home to whom they reported results. Partnership would affect them all and complicate not only their busy lives, but also management back at headquarters.

If it's difficult to practice partnership in our own backyard, it's even more difficult across international borders. While much is happening that is positive, partnership remains the dream, rather than the practice, of many missions. Some mission leaders are afraid of organizationally partnering with non-Western agencies. They fear the effects upon their own well-run established organizations; they remember past history when others went through great difficulties as they developed partnerships; they fear repercussions.

Several years ago Dr. Donald McGavran called together all the agencies based in southern California who work in India. This included national as well as Western bodies. McGavran challenged their isolationism and urged them to develop cooperative efforts to reach India. Discussions were friendly and enthusiastic, but one who was there recalls, "the minute the glow of the conference was finished, each one started to gravitate back to his normal state of work."

Dr. Dale Kietzman, until recently executive vice president of the William Carey University at the U.S. Center for World Mission, and former Wycliffe missionary, questions whether partnership with Two-Thirds World agencies is working very well. He says:

> You still have a certain amount of paternalism involved in that, because the North American agencies can afford to assign personnel and offer to do things that the Third-World agencies cannot afford to do. . . . Too often I feel that the North American agencies are tending to take the lead when they shouldn't.

Obstacles to Partnership
As we've looked at many models of partnership, the benefits and synergism have become obvious. But obstacles that hinder partnering remain.

Western agencies may struggle with:

☐ A spirit of competition between themselves as they need a greater share of the Christian dollar to carry out their own program.

☐ Pride in organization . . . desire to be known as "leaders in the field."

☐ Proliferation of organizations; too many Christian entrepreneurs want to lead their own organizations rather than offer their idea to complement another organization.

☐ Fear of losing control and not being able to continue operating from the same power base.

☐ Fear of losing reason for existence if the partner agency becomes larger and stronger and can "go it alone." (Even missionaries may reject giving nationals more responsibility and control for fear they may no longer be needed.)

☐ Lack of trust of national leadership because of a misunderstanding of cultural differences and expectations.

Some national ministries resist partnering with the West because they:

☐ Fear they will lose control under the power of Western money and the dominance of Western leadership.

☐ Don't want to lose the indigenous character of their ministry. For many it is a distinct disadvantage to their outreach to be known as a "puppet of the West."

☐ Still harbor feelings of resentment and bitterness over past mission/church and racial tensions.

☐ Have misperceptions of what partnership involves; feel accountability and report requirements are indications of paternalism.

Even partnerships between Two-Thirds World agencies face obstacles such as:

☐ Not enough good models in practice for them to observe and pattern after.

☐ Nationals needing to develop deeper trust relationships between themselves. The strong tribal ties which were so beneficial in their history, today tend to affect relationships negatively. Extended family and tribal loyalties may militate against choices of leadership based on gifts and abilities.

☐ The inferiority complex many nationals acquired during colonial rule has swung the pendulum so that some nationals want to be their "own man" rather than backing and being a part of someone else's program.

☐ Government financial restrictions make it very difficult to send money out of many Two-Thirds World countries, limiting the extent of the partnership an agency can develop.

Test the Cords

How can you determine whether an agency is truly partnering and committed to cooperative ministries? Some agencies may have such a specialized ministry in a specific location that partnership is not practical at this point. For example, a church-planting ministry in an unreached country may not have a church with which to partner for some time, and even then, emerging leadership would only gradually be trained and prepared for a partnership commitment.

No one model of partnership has, or probably ever will, emerge as the best, so not all the criteria of partnership may apply to each one. Effective partnerships are tailor-made to the needs and situation of the partners involved. But the following list of questions will help you to think about the direction the mission or national ministry is taking and whether partnership is merely a principle espoused publicly or taken seriously in practice.

1. Does the mission's written statements of policy indicate that partnership is part of its goal?

2. Are partner representatives involved in discussions and decision-making on issues in which they are affected, even at the board level?

3. If you are considering going to the field, will the mission put you in touch with key national partners so you can communicate

directly with them concerning relationships, goals and strategies?

4. How is partnership practiced in relation to the ten ingredients of partnership discussed in chapters 4 and 5?

5. Are there written partnership agreements? Do these include financial policies and standards of accountability for both?

6. Is the mission consulting with, meeting and planning with other churches or parachurch organizations, both national and Western, in the field?

7. Is there any evidence that the mission is promoting, praising or encouraging prayer for ministries outside its own?

8. From all you know of this mission would you say it is spending more effort promoting its own kingdom than the kingdom of God?

When You're Disappointed
We have found at Partners International that even with a determined effort to be good partners on our part, and the best intentions of our partner ministries, partnership does not always work smoothly. The old nature, unfortunately, allows jealousy, selfishness, pride and all those other unlovely characteristics to mar the relationships. We must constantly upgrade our levels of trust. We ought to ask for forgiveness more and contextualize our judgments. Working with national ministries in almost fifty countries stretches our flexibility to the utmost.

As a donor, missions committee member, church leader or candidate, you will also find that partnership will not meet up to all your expectations.

☐ Your expectations are probably too idealistic. North American Christians romanticize and idealize missions as they do marriage. Missionaries are saints; nationals are super-spiritual; the national church glorifies God through suffering.

Be realistic and accept the fact that missionaries and national leaders are as subject to human frailties as you are and that partners in missions, as partners in marriage, don't always work in harmony.

We're going to find many models. Some will work; some won't. We have to be free to fail. Let's not force partnerships or insist that all be integrated into one.

☐ Try to understand the difference in communication between Western and Two-Thirds Worlds before judging the partnership too harshly. Some cultures are even less oriented to written communication than ours (and ours is fast becoming visual and oral rather than written). Without the infrastructure of telephone, fax, secretaries and equipment, the communications we demand can become a heavy burden. Don't become discouraged if letters or reports are not always on time or are incomplete.

☐ Allow room for crosscultural differences. Leadership styles, decision-making processes and financial accountability are culturally affected. In some cultures, for example, it is well understood that extended family members should be given positions of responsibility in an organization, for they are most likely to be dependable and trustworthy.

In financial matters "designation" may not have nearly the significance as "need." In a partnership, of course, established and acceptable policies must be followed, but it may take time for both partners to truly understand the outworking of those policies. Don't be quick to misjudge a partnership in areas that may have crosscultural ramifications.

Signs of Victory

As donors, prayer partners, mission leaders and nationals all see the urgency of cooperation and partnership, we will no doubt learn of more victories in this arena.

The British professor can rejoice that there are exciting signs of partnership among the parachurch youth ministries today, some of whom no doubt were part of the twenty-nine campus organizations.

The presidents and their spouses of six major youth ministries (InterVarsity, Young Life, Navigators, Youth for Christ, Fellowship of Christian Athletes and Campus Crusade for Christ) meet twice a year for prayer. Several of these organizations have wide overseas ministries as well as their North American programs. Dr. Steve Hayner, president of InterVarsity, reported in his newsletter (May 1990), "I see these times as vital for me as I work on partnership in the gospel with these organizations."

These six presidents had joined together to celebrate the fiftieth anniversary of Young Life a few months earlier. As the six men stood together on the platform, many in the audience were moved to tears. Dr. Bill Bright of Campus Crusade later wrote:

Many stated that the highlight of the conference was the testimony of the six of us, standing together, united in Christ. . . . It was not always this way. The walls were impenetrable years ago, and little communication existed between individuals of various Christian groups or between organizations or denominations. I first noticed these barriers shortly after I came to know Christ personally forty-five years ago.

Since then, there has been a dramatic movement of God's Spirit. In his sovereign, loving way, God has been tearing down the spiritual Berlin Walls. Through the enabling of his spirit, he is causing believers to love one another and to worship him together. He is showing us the need that each believer and organization and denomination has for the other.[1]

We rejoice that we are clearly entering a new era of partnership in Christian circles, not only in the West, but between the Western and non-Western world. The responsibility to evangelize is being taken up by the "whole body of Christ." More Christians from more countries are seeking to fulfill the Great Commission than at any time in history. The promise of unprecedented spiritual harvest and of seeing the remaining unreached people reached with the gospel looms tantalizingly before us. Today, perhaps even more than in Paul's day, we rejoice because of the partnerships in the gospel that are being formed around this globe, these beautiful cords of victory.

Appendix 1

Partners International Sample Working Agreement

Principles and Guidelines for Cooperative Work Between Partner Ministry and CNEC, Partners International (CNEC-PI)

CNEC—Partners International exists to participate with Christian ministries throughout the world to fulfill the Great Commission. This is accomplished through the means of complementary partnership—the mutual sharing of vision, knowledge, wisdom, expertise and material resources.

In order to establish an effective partnership, both CNEC-PI and the partner ministry must have a firm understanding about what the assistance program is to accomplish, for whom, and by what methods. The means for achieving these understandings and establishing necessary safeguards is the Working Agreement.

The Working Agreement has three parts: (1) Principles of Partnership, (2) Policies for Cooperative Work, and (3) Guidelines for Cooperative Work. Principles and Policies represent the basic values which must be held in common by both partners and without which complementary partnerships would be impossible. Guidelines for cooperative work are those elements which are unique to a particular partnership and which are designed by mutual agreement.

Principles of Partnership

As those who share in God's grace with each other (Phil 1:7); who have been qualified to share in the inheritance of the saints in the Kingdom of light (Col 1:12); who share in the heavenly calling (Heb 6:4); who share in His holiness (Heb 12:10); and as those who also will share in the glory to be revealed (1 Pet 5:1), we as partners in the work of God affirm:

1. That we are called to invest our lives and resources in Christ's ministry of reconciliation (2 Cor 5:18);

2. That God has given His church a variety of gifts to complement each other in the ministry of equipping it to fulfill its mandate for the glory of Christ (Eph 4:11-13);

3. That in seeking to fulfill this mandate, we recognize that our enablement does not depend on human criteria such as wealth, education, experience, and other attributes, but on the Holy Spirit (Zech 4:6);

4. That it is both an honor and an obligation for Christians to assist one another in the work of Christ (2 Cor 8);

5. That any God-honoring service should be carried out in a spirit of mutual respect, trust and submission to the Lord (Col 3:24); Gal 5:13); 6. That mutual accountability is an integral aspect of Christian stewardship (1 Cor 4:2; Rom 14:12); and

7. That our motivation should be that of a servant in keeping with the example of Christ (Phil 2).

Policies for Cooperative Work

CNEC-PI holds partnership in missions to be the temporary affiliation of independent ministries by which one serves to fill out or complete the other within the framework of a common goal. In support of this position CNEC-PI works exclusively with:

1. Autonomous ministries that subscribe to the foundational doctrines of Scripture as set forth in the CNEC-PI Statement of Faith.

2. Autonomous ministries that are overseen by a duly constituted national body or board.

3. Autonomous ministries that see themselves and CNEC-PI as independent of the other, and agree that neither should interfere in the administration of the other.

4. Autonomous ministries that are willing to work within the framework of a Working Agreement which is drawn up through a collaborative process between CNEC-PI and the partner ministry.

CNEC—Partners International

In cooperation with the partner ministry, CNEC-PI is committed to:

1. Pursuing with integrity a policy of complementary assistance to the partner ministry and its members.

2. Publishing its audited financial report annually and sending a copy to the partner ministry upon request.

3. Honoring the donor's intent by transferring all funds as designated with the understanding that overhead funds are included.

4. Giving a full explanation of its relationship with other missions in any publicity so as not to confuse God's people with unclear reporting, nor to discredit or violate the indigenous nature of the partner ministry.

5. Fostering a continuing prayer burden for the partner ministry and a financial interest in it by making available all information about the ministry, assisting the development of a donor base, and arranging deputation programs if and when necessary.

6. Defining all matters of planning and evaluating its involvement with the partner ministry.

7. Contributing to the self-developing capabilities of the partner ministry.

Partner Ministry

In cooperation with CNEC-PI the partner ministry is committed to:

1. Negotiating a Working Agreement and maintaining the partnership according to the agreed-upon framework.

2. Negotiating all new projects with CNEC-PI, where such help is needed, so as to avoid obligating CNEC-PI to any projects not duly approved for funding.

3. Providing an audited financial report annually to CNEC-PI's International President.

4. Keeping CNEC-PI fully informed of the general situation of its ministry and the progress of the specific assistance program.

5. Permitting CNEC-PI to represent and publicize the projects assisted by CNEC-PI, providing there is no likelihood of adverse effect to the partner ministry.

6. Informing the associated councils when partner ministry personnel travel in those countries where CNEC-PI has an associated council.

7. Working under the established deputation program when speakers are invited by CNEC-PI to go abroad to promote ministry projects.

8. Maintaining the indigenous nature of the ministry and strengthening its self-developing capabilities.

Guidelines for Cooperative Work

Whereas God has led CNEC—Partners International (CNEC-PI), located at 1470 North Fourth Street, San Jose, California 95112, and (PARTNER MINISTRY) (PARTNER), located at (ADDRESS:), (COUNTRY:) to work cooperatively for the advancement of the Kingdom of God, the following guidelines are hereby set forth:

1. CNEC-PI will provide assistance to the following elements of the (PARTNER) program:

(ELEMENTS OF MINISTRY TO BE SPONSORED/FUNDED:)

2. The purpose and over-all goals of these elements of the ministry are:

(PURPOSE, GOALS:)

3. The (operational) plans for the next (LENGTH OF PERIOD OF VALIDITY OF THIS WORKING AGREEMENT:) years in order to reach these goals are: (PLANS:)

4. The expected outcomes to be achieved as a result of the carrying out of these plans are: (OUTCOMES EXPECTED:)

5. CNEC-PI will transfer funds for (ALLOCATION:) as well as for projects agreed upon by CNEC-PI and (PARTNER). These funds shall be transferred to the board of (PARTNER) in (COUNTRY) through a mutually agreed upon method. All such projects must be documented through the Project Request form or through

authorized correspondence. (PARTNER) will distribute all funds as designated.

6. (PARTNER) will provide CNEC-PI with an annually-audited financial report within four months of the close of the fiscal year. Each report will include a schedule detailing CNEC-PI donations which corresponds to the Income and Expense Statement. The financial report will be prepared by an external audit if CNEC-PI donations exceed U.S. $20,000 annually.

7. (PARTNER) will provide CNEC-PI with a copy of its annual budget no later than one month after the onset of the fiscal year. Each budget should include anticipated expenses and income with CNEC-PI listed as a subcategory.

8. (PARTNER) will provide the reports and information necessary for CNEC-PI services, fund-raising and representation as outlined in the Ministry Information report. The information required for worker support includes photographs, testimonies, and personal data on all workers receiving CNEC-PI assistance. Every worker shall provide prayer letters or field reports at least three times per year (specifically in January, May and September).

If a prayer letter or field report is not received from any worker by the deadline, and no explanation is given, funds for that worker or work will be withheld from the monthly allocation until such time as a letter or report is received in the CNEC-PI office. (PARTNER) also agrees to provide CNEC-PI with periodic reports and photos of any mutual short-term projects.

9. CNEC-PI will maintain a mailing list on behalf of (PARTNER) for all contacts outside of (COUNTRY). CNEC-PI and (PARTNER) will keep each other informed of any communications to individuals or groups on this mailing list. No worker of (PARTNER) will appeal to sponsors for contributions towards projects or needs unapproved by the (PARTNER) board and the International Coordinating Office.

10. Individuals within CNEC-PI and the organization of (PARTNER) will be made aware of the working relationship between CNEC-PI and (PARTNER), and encouraged to pray for the worldwide fellowship of CNEC-PI.

11. Both CNEC-PI and (PARTNER) agree that this Working Agreement is subject to review at any time and at least by (MONTH, YEAR:).

(NAME)	Luis Bush
(TITLE)	International President
(PARTNER MINISTRY)	CNEC—Partners International

(NAME)	Alexandre C. Araujo
(TITLE)	International Ministries
(PARTNER MINISTRY)	CNEC—Partners International
Date:_____	Date:_____

Appendix 2

Partner Mission Agreement between the Indian Evangelical Mission and Sudan Interior Mission International

Partner Mission Agreement between the Indian Evangelical Mission (hereinafter referred to as IEM) and Sudan Interior Mission International (hereinafter referred to as SIM)

Preamble

The IEM and SIM seeks to establish a Partner-Mission relationship to work together in the recruitment and support of cross-cultural missionaries to serve in the fields of Africa and South America (where SIM operates) to achieve mutual goals in evangelism, church-planting, teaching and supportive ministries to the Glory of God. In accordance with this Partner Mission agreement, the IEM and SIM agree to administer cooperative ministries as follows:

Member Missionary Relationship:

1. The missionary shall have dual membership status with both the IEM and SIM.

2. The appointment of the missionary shall be subject to the approval of both agencies in accordance with the standards established by each agency.

3. In the event that the other agency requests confidential materials gathered by the other, such materials shall be shared with the understanding that the materials shall be kept confidential by that agency.

4. The missionary candidate shall participate in the full candidate and training program of both agencies.

5. Sufficient time shall be allowed for deputation work under the coordination of the IEM (in India) and SIM (outside India) in order that adequate prayer and financial support can be realized.

6. SIM shall supervise the securing of visas and make other arrangements needful for the beginning of field work.

7. The IEM shall be the sending agency for financial and prayer support of the missionary. In view of the special financial situation in India SIM will endeavor to

raise external financial support as detailed in Clause 15.

8. SIM shall be the directing agency in relation to missionary activities on the field and financial care.

9. While on the field, and while traveling to and from the field, the missionary shall be under the jurisdiction of the SIM.

10. While on the field, the missionary shall be an integral part of the field staff sharing equally in privileges, responsibilities as any other member and being subject to the policies and direction of SIM.

11. The missionary's field director will initiate furlough planning in consultation with the IEM and SIM East Asia office.

12. While on furlough, the missionary shall be under the jurisdiction of the IEM. Among the missionary's furlough responsibilities, consideration will be given by IEM to assignments, projects, additional study or training requested by SIM. Progress reports and information during furlough will be provided to SIM.

13. While on furlough the missionary shall primarily carry on a deputation ministry for the IEM within the constituency of the IEM congregations. When requested by SIM to undertake additional deputation or activities such expenses shall be SIM's responsibility.

14. The missionary shall not solicit for personal funds from home or field constituencies of either agency without the permission of the respective agency.

15.1 The financial support of the missionary will be the mutual responsibility of the IEM and SIM.

15.2 IEM shall endeavor to raise funds to meet the outgoing needs (one-way airfare costs, baggage allowance, equipment needs, etc.) and to set up financial plans to take care of home medical and accommodation needs whilst on furlough and also retirement/insurance schemes.

15.3 SIM will raise financial support for IEM missionaries from Churches and Christians in Asia and other countries to cover Field's support, medical and accommodation, return airfare, and administrative costs. All IEM/SIM missionary appointees shall not leave for the Field until their outgoing funds and 90% of their external financial support have been raised. All IEM/SIM missionaries must be available, prior to moving to the fields, for deputation in other Asian Countries where support is being raised.

15.4 The support allowance for IEM missionaries will be the same as that for all other SIM members.

15.5 Whilst the missionary is in the field SIM shall take care of support allowances, medical, housing and other needs.

16. When the missionary is on furlough the IEM shall be responsible for the salary allowance & home care costs (medical and housing) according to IEM Salary structure as well as the return airfare to the field after furlough.

17. The IEM missionaries recommended for service with SIM would fully accept

the SIM Manual including the Doctrinal Statement on page 4, and agree to live and serve in accord with the policies and practices contained therein. As an integrated Mission SIM does not have separate national or denominational areas of work.

Administrative Matters:

18. The SIM East Asia office in Singapore is responsible for all SIM's relationships with countries in South-East Asia, the Far East and India.

19. The IEM will cooperate with SIM East Asia in the following:

a. Candidates:

☐ notify prospective candidates of service opportunities and giving full information.

☐ all enquirers will be dealt directly through the office of the General Secretary of the IEM.

☐ the Mission Board of IEM will screen, interview and appoint the candidates as IEM missionaries and then second them to work with SIM. In doing so, the IEM will accept the norms set up by SIM for its candidates.

☐ prior to their appointment, the IEM will inform SIM and await confirmation of service opportunity from SIM East Asia.

☐ following acceptance by SIM, the IEM will be responsible for final preparation for service in the field in cooperation with SIM.

b. Missionaries:

☐ when in India, they will come under the direction of the IEM concerning furlough arrangements, additional training, deputation, etc., but all matters relating to their status as SIM missionary are to be discussed with SIM.

☐ when in the field, they will come under the direction of the SIM Area Director or International Liaison Officer (ILO): according to SIM's relationship with the National Church in the particular country.

☐ will receive SIM monthly salary allowance and copies of reports and prayer letters will be sent to the IEM, SIM Area and National offices.

20. The IEM will receive from SIM:

☐ regular information concerning SIM programs

☐ copies of "SIM-NOW" magazine and other literatures as appropriate

☐ lists of vacancies in the field—approximately bi-monthly

☐ lists of approved financial needs from the field—approximately bi-monthly

☐ end of term reports on IEM missionaries

☐ open communication concerning all matters relating to IEM personnel

☐ annual assessment of total support requirement for each missionary for the following financial year (October 1 to September 30)

21. The IEM and SIM Area Offices:

a. All missionary assignments are made by the Area Council in the field or National Church and are communicated through the SIM East Asia office.

b. Length of term/furlough will be agreed with the Area Director on the ILO. The length of term for IEM/SIM missionaries is normally four years with twelve months' furlough.

c. The missionary is responsible to the Area Director or ILO concerning all matters relating to his ministry and service in the field. The IEM will be informed well in advance before a missionary is transferred from one ministry to another except in an emergency.

d. Any correspondence from the IEM to the SIM Area Office should be copied to the SIM East Asia office.

THE TENURE OF THIS AGREEMENT WOULD BE 5 (FIVE) YEARS AFTER WHICH IT WOULD BE REVIEWED AND RENEWED.

SIGNED:

General Secretary, East Asia General Secretary
Sudan Interior Mission International Indian Evangelical Mission

Appendix 3

Great Commission Manifesto

January 8, 1989
Singapore

We, the 314 participants from 50 nations gathered for the Global Consultation for World Evangelization by A.D. 2000 and Beyond, come from many different churches, denominations and ministries under the direction of the Holy Spirit for what we consider to be a singular moment in the history of the Church.

We identify ourselves as a gathering of Christians who by faith alone have accepted Jesus Christ, true God and true man, revealed in the infallible and holy Scriptures as our Lord and Savior. We are committed to biblical righteousness in our behavior and to growth in holiness.

We gratefully acknowledge the worldwide witness and ministry of faithful men and women throughout the previous twenty centuries.

We humbly confess our pride, prejudice, competition and disobedience that have hindered our generation from effectively working at the task of world evangelization. These sins have impeded God's desire to spread abroad His gracious provision of eternal salvation through the precious blood of His Son, Jesus Christ.

We turn from these sins and failures to express our belief that God has graciously opened to us a window of opportunity for completing the magnificent task He has given us. We boldly seize this crucial moment, more impressed with God's great power than any force arrayed against us.

Cooperation and Partnership

We have listened to each other and rejoice at what God is doing through many plans for world evangelization. We learned that there are over 2000 separate plans relating to world evangelization.

We see afresh that cooperation and partnership are absolute necessities if the Great Commission is going to be fulfilled by the Year 2000. For the sake of those who are lost and eternally separated from God, we have dared to pray and dream of what might happen if appropriate autonomy of churches and ministries could be balanced with significant partnership.

Empowerment
We acknowledge that the evangelization of the world can be carried out only in the power of the Holy Spirit. Listening and ready, we declare our dependence upon the Holy Spirit and commit to undergird all efforts for world evangelization with personal and corporate prayer. We recognize that human energy cannot replace divine activity nor can spiritual success be measured in terms of human achievement. The effectiveness of our endeavors does not lie in human expertise but in the sovereign activity of the Holy Spirit.

Compassion
The Good News of Jesus Christ brings special meaning to suffering humanity. God's love brings hope to those who live under the bondage of sin, and who are victims of poverty and injustice. We believe that Christians involved in world evangelization should live among people as servants and minister to the needs of the whole person.

Toward Fulfillment
The revelation of God in Christ is plain. The commission to His Church is clear. The unfinished task is apparent. The opportunity to work together is ours.

We believe that it is possible to bring the Gospel to all people by the year 2000. This can be accomplished with sufficient dedication, unity, and mobilization of available resources, powered and directed by God.

To accomplish this objective, it will be necessary to:

1. Focus particularly on those who have not yet heard the Gospel.

2. Provide every people and population on earth with a valid opportunity to hear the Gospel in a language they can understand. It is our fervent prayer that at least half of humanity will profess allegiance to the Lord Jesus.

3. Establish a mission-minded church planting movement within every unreached people group so that the Gospel is accessible to all people.

4. Establish a Christian community of worship, instruction in the word, healing, fellowship, prayer, disciple making, evangelism, and missionary concern in every human community.

To God Be The Glory For All He Enables Us To Do By The End Of This Millennium!

Notes

Chapter One: Partnerships Everywhere

[1]Lois Rosenthal, *Partnering, A Guide to Co-Owning Anything from Homes to Home Computers* (Cincinnati, Ohio: Writer's Digest Books, 1983).

[2]Cheri Fuller, "How to Improve the Parent Teacher Connection," *Focus on the Family,* September 1989, p. 2.

[3]Louis Kroar, "Your Rivals Can Be Your Allies," in *Fortune,* March 27, 1989.

Chapter Two: Partnering Goes Back a Long Way

[1]George Peters, *A Biblical Theology of Missions* (Chicago: Moody Press), pp. 234-35.

Chapter Three: From Paternalism to Partnership

[1]Walbert Buhlmann, *The Coming of the Third Church* (Maryknoll, N.Y.: Orbis, 1977), p. 23.

Chapter Four: It Sounds Like a Marriage

[1]David Fraser, ed., *The Church in New Frontiers for Mission* (Monrovia, Calif.: MARC, 1983).

Chapter Six: The Daughter Becomes a Friend

[1]George Peters, ed., *Missions in Creative Tension,* p. 196.

Chapter Seven: Mainline Models

[1]Larry Keyes, *The Last Age of Missions* (Pasadena, Calif.: William Carey Library, 1983), p. 11.

[2]Winston Crawley, *Global Mission* (Nashville: Broadman, 1985), p. 382.

Chapter Eight: Crucified Nationalism

[1]John Naisbitt and Patricia Aburdene, *Megatrends 2000* (New York: William Morrow, 1990), p. 131.

[2]Patrick Johnstone, "The World Evangelized by 2000—But at What Cost?" *World*

Evangelization, May-June 1989, p. 21.
[3]Eun Mou Lee, "West and East Must Get Along—A Korean Missionary Speaks Out," *Evangelical Missions Quarterly,* July 1983, p. 193.
[4]Gerald and Barbara Wibberly, "The Normal Missionary Life," *East Asia's Millions,* January-February 1990, p. 302.

Chapter Nine: Great Expectations
[1]Christopher Robinson, "A Study of Financial Statement Ratios of Member Organizations of the EFCA," unpublished dissertation, College of Professional Studies, University of San Francisco, December 1989.

Chapter Ten: Testing the Waters
[1]Larry Pate, *From Every People* (Monrovia, Calif.: MARC, 1989), pp. 50-52.
[2]Larry Keyes, *The Last Age of Missions* (Pasadena, Calif.: William Carey Library, 1983), p. 85.
[3]David Cho, ed., "The Third Force," *The Official Report of the Third Triennial Convention of the Asia Missions Association,* Seoul, 1982.
[4]Jung Woong Kim, "Third World Mission—Church Relationship: A Korean-Thai Model," unpublished dissertation, Trinity Evangelical Divinity School, Deerfield, Ill., 1985, p. 163.
[5]Ibid., p. 121.

Chapter Twelve: Global Glue
[1]Thomas Wong, ed., *Countdown to A.D. 2000,* A. D. 2000 Movement, 1989, pp. 93-94

Chapter Thirteen: Into the Next Century
[1]Tom Housten and Thomas Wang, "A Joint Statement from the Lausanne Committee for World Evangelization and the A.D. 2000 Movement," *A.D. 2000 and Beyond,* vol. 1, no. 1, January-February 1990, p. 4.
[2]Ibid., p. 4.

Chapter Fifteen: The Cords of Victory
[1]Bill Bright, "Brightside," Campus Crusade for Christ newsletter for staff and alumni, February 1990.